Floral Diversity and Ecosystem Function in Northeast India

Floral Diversity And Ecosystem Function In Northeast India

Jenpuiru Kamei

AKANSHA PUBLISHING HOUSE
NEW DELHI • GUWAHATI • VISAKHAPATNAM

AKANSHA PUBLISHING HOUSE
4649-B/21, Ansari Road
Darya Ganj, New Delhi - 110 002
Ph.: 23263193 / 9811582579 / 09435116718
Fax: 011-23263193
Email: ektabooks@yahoo.com
www.akanshapublishinghouse.com

Floral Diversity and Ecosystem Function in Northeast India

First Published 2010

ISBN 978-81-8370-251-5

PRINTED IN INDIA

Published by Akansha Publishing House, New Delhi and Printed at Harmain Offset Press, Delhi.

Contents

Preface

This work is based on my doctoral dissertation submitted to North-eastern Hill University, Shillong and approved in the year 2008. I worked under the able guidance of Prof. H. N. Pandey of Centre for Advanced Studies in Botany, NEHU and Prof. S.K. Barik of the same centre.

I worked in the village of Swer in East Khasi Hills district of Meghalaya state where there are well protected sacred groves of the indigenous Khasi people. I am lucky that the head man of the village, Mr. Orstar Swer extended full co-operation to me.

As is well known, Meghalaya is a part of ecosystem of northeast India which is a hot spot of biodiversity. I worked on the inter-relationship between tree diversity and ecosystem function.

I have already published three papers churned out of this work in the following journals: 1. *Canadian Journal of Forest Research,* 2009, Vol. 39-47. 2. *ANVEṢĀ Journal of Fakir Mohan University*, 2008, Vol. 3(1):1-10

I am grateful to the Editors of *Candadian Journal of Forest Research* and *ANVEṢĀ* for their kind publication of my papers. Simultaneously I express my gratefulness to *Canadian Journal of Forest Research* for their kind permission to reproduce the article in the present book. I was greatly helped by my two teachers Prof. H.N. Pandey and Prof. S.K. Barik in the publication of these three papers.

In the preparation of this work, I got help from many of my colleagues in the Centre for Advanced Studies in Botany, NEHU. However, I would like to mention Dr. Krishna Upadhaya and Dr. N.J. Lakadong.

I also acknowledge the financial assistance given to me by UGC-DSA programme and UGC Rajiv Gandhi National Fellowship.

I am grateful to my father Prof. Gangmumei Kamei for giving me guidance and cooperation. I am extremely grateful to Mr. M.P. Misra, Managing Director of Akansha Publishing House, New Delhi for agreeing to publish this work. I also thank Editor of Ms. Akansha Publishing House who is responsible for making the book in the present form.

Jenpuiru Kamei

Imphal
Dated 1st June, 2010

1

Introduction

The most striking feature of the earth's biota is its extraordinary diversity, estimated to include about 10 million different species. Of the estimated 2,97,000–5,10,000 plant species of the world's biota (Schippmann *et al.* 2002), only 1,70,000 have been described to date (Groombridge and Jenkins 2000), and their distribution is highly uneven. About seven per cent of the world's total land area is home to half of the world's species, with the tropics alone accounting for 5 million.

India contributes significantly to this latitudinal biodiversity trend. A rich and varied heritage of biodiversity, encompassing a wide spectrum of habitats from tropical rainforests to alpine vegetation and from savanna to coastal wetlands is encountered in the country. There are nearly 47,000 species of plants, which includes 17,000 angiosperms (Trivedi 2002), accounting for 10.78% of the global total. Of the 17,000 species of flowering plants, 5,725 are endemic to the Indian subcontinent accounting for 33.5% of the total flora, of which, 2,532 are restricted to the Himalayas. The Red Data Books (Jain and Shastry 1984; Nayar and Shastry 1988–90) list 623 threatened species of which 550 are endemic including some valuable medicinal plants.

The vegetation of northeastern India has 1,63,799 km^2 area under forest accounting for 25% of the total forest cover of the country (FSI 1999), and harbours approximately 7,500 species of angiosperms. Meghalaya in northeast India with an actual forest cover of around 15,584 km^2 (FSI 2001) harbours about 3,128 species of flowering plants and contributes about 18% of the total flora of the country. It includes 1,237 endemic species (Khan *et al.* 1997) and 53 threatened plant species (Nayar and Sastry 1988). In Meghalaya, very few studies are available on endemic and threatened plant species. Most of these species are restricted to Biosphere Reserves, National Parks, Wild Life Sanctuary, community and reserved forest, and sacred groves.

Sacred groves are small patches of forest protected by local people out of reverence and respect, fear and sentiment. They are the home of the local flora and fauna. Tree felling and hunting of animals are strictly prohibited here. Leaves, fruits or roots may be removed only for medicinal purposes. Ecologically the sacred groves represent the climax vegetation of the area. In Meghalaya, it ranges from moist deciduous forests at lower elevation to subtropical semi-evergreen to evergreen forest in the precipitous zone at higher elevation between 1200–1900 m a.s.l.

Forests in India have been and are being exploited intensely for centuries (Veach *et al.* 2003). Although the degree of anthropogenic pressure varies in different parts of the country, human disturbances have become a wide spread feature in most of the forested areas throughout the Himalayas (Singh *et al.* 1984). In the northeastern region, dependence on forest for fuelwood as a source of energy, coupled with shifting cultivation has been causing deforestation (Ramakrishnan 1987). Due to the ever-increasing population, fuelwood consumption is also increasing rapidly in the region (Arunachalam *et al.* 2004). In Meghalaya, the main causes of biodiversity loss are shifting cultivation, deforestation, mining, habitat destruction, over extraction, fragmentation and land use changes (SoE 2005). Lately, the pressure on forests in the state has increased many folds leading to encroachment in sacred groves by the indigenous tribes themselves for their various needs.

The biodiversity declines are already pronounced in many areas. Such local declines are often even more dramatic than global declines, and the beneficial effects of many organisms on local processes are lost long before the species become globally extinct (Naeem *et al.* 1999).

Human modifications to the living community in an ecosystem as well as to the collective biodiversity have a strong potential to alter ecological properties, ecosystem goods and services which they provide to humanity. Therefore, ecologists have raised concern about how a change in species diversity alters functioning of the ecosystem such as productivity and processes leading to transfer of C and nutrients within the ecosystem and its stability.

An understanding of the relationship between biological diversity and functioning of ecosystems can help improve a wide range of policies involving agriculture, forestry, fisheries and land use, transcending traditional conservation-based policies (Mooney *et al.* 1995). Although every organism contributes to ecosystem processes, the nature and magnitude of individual contributions vary considerably. An understanding of the ecosystem level consequences of individual species is also essential to examine the interactions between biological diversity and ecosystem function. If we cannot establish that individual species are significant, we are unlikely to be able to detect the much more subtle and complex effects of species diversity. Individual species matter, or at least some of them do, and the loss or gain of those species alters the net effects of terrestrial ecosystem on the atmosphere, the hydrosphere or the long-term fertility of soils (Ehrlich and Mooney 1983).

When discussing the effects of biodiversity on ecosystem function it is important to be specific about which components of biodiversity are affecting which components of functioning. Variation in ecosystem properties can result from fluctuations in the environment from year to year, directional changes in conditions, abiotic disturbance or biotic disturbance. There is no a priori reason to expect that different ecosystem properties have a single pattern of response to changes in different components of biodiversity, or that change in either direction is inherently "good" or "bad" (Hooper *et al.* 2005).

The natural forest is never homogenous in structure; it is always an irregular mosaic of developing and developed stages of community, often called as gap, building and mature phases. The young, mature and senescent individuals of most tree species are unevenly distributed and cause patchiness in the forest structure and composition (Richards 1996). The forest vegetation produces a complex 3-dimensional mosaic of microclimates varying vertically from canopy top to the forest floor and horizontally from point to point beneath the canopy. At a larger scale, microclimates vary between canopy gaps of different sizes, between building and mature phases, and between different forest types. Each of the contrasting microclimates has a role to play in accounting for biology of individual plants and animals in the forest.

The structure and function of forest ecosystem is determined by the plant component more than any other living component of the system. The importance of plant control at the ecosystem level lies in driving nutrient cycling back to the plants. This is possible due to the high proportion of total stock of nutrients that is held in shoot system and the "leak-proof" efficiency of the forest floor and soil compartments of the ecosystem (Richards 1996).

The flow of nutrients within the forest ecosystems occurs through: 1) root nutrient absorption via the processes of uptake and assimilation, 2) nutrient allocation to biomass construction and maintenance, 3) nutrient translocation from senescent tissue, 4) return of nutrients in above and below ground litter and 5) microbially mediated release of inorganic nutrients into soils solution i.e. mineralization during organic matter decomposition (Barnes *et al.* 1998).

Nutrients entering forest ecosystem from mineral weathering, atmospheric deposition and biological fixation can enter soil solution where they are absorbed by plant roots. Within the plant, absorbed nutrients participate in a wide array of physiological processes, and in some cases, nutrients are mobilized (i.e., translocated) prior to the shedding of some plant tissues. Plant litter on the forest floor plays a critical role in determining soil properties and substrate supply for microorganisms. Most of the nutrients leaving the aboveground biomass as litter or as leachates reach the forest floor rapidly, where soil microorganisms decompose them. The decomposition of litter by microbes into inorganic ions and turnover of labile soil organic matter is affected by the litter quality and timing of litter input, besides microenvironmental conditions on the forest floor. During the process of decomposition, soil bacteria, actinomycetes and fungi assimilate the organic compounds contained in plant litter into their cells for biosynthesis i.e., growth and maintenance. In humid tropical forest dense networks of fine roots, which are concentrated on the forest floor and the underlying mineral soil layer, rapidly absorb ecosystem nutrients released during decomposition of litter. Thus, the rate at which nutrients flow within the forest ecosystems is controlled by the physiological activities of plants and soil microorganisms, and their requirement for growth.

Although microbial biomass represents a relatively small standing stock of nutrients compared to soil organic matter and above ground biomass of trees, but act as a labile source of nutrients for plants, a pathway for incorporation of organic matter into the soil, and a temporary sink for nutrients. The soil microbes associated with tree species differing in quality of leaf litter often have variable amounts of microbial biomass (Bauhas *et al.* 1998), rates of decomposition of organic matter (Melillo *et al.* 1982), mineralization (Vitousek *et al.* 1982, Zak and Pregitzer 1990) and nitrification (Finzi *et al.* 1998a, Lovette and Reuth 1999). The phenological diversity of trees in the forest helps reduce nutrient loss from the system by allowing plant uptake to take place concurrently with microbial mineralization (Baillie 1996).

In forest ecosystems, major pathways of nutrient losses are through leaching and denitrification. Leaching of growth limiting nutrients like N and P in particular occurs when precipitation exceeds the amount of water lost through transpiration and evaporation from the soil surface. Nutrients eventually enter ground or surface waters where they then become a nutrient input for aquatic ecosystems. Denitrification, on the other hand, is the microbially mediated reduction of nitrate to nitrous oxide or nitrogen, which returns N to the atmosphere (Tiedje 1988). This results in the loss of limiting nutrients, potentially influencing the productivity of terrestrial ecosystems.

The focus of ecological research over the past decade has been on the study of relationship between biodiversity and ecosystem functioning (Schulze and Mooney 1993). However, ecologists have different views on the importance of species diversity in ecosystem functioning because empirical studies have not demonstrated any consistent relationship between the number of species in a system and the rates of ecological processes. Several studies have provided clear evidence that biological communities do indeed regulate ecological processes (Tilman *et al.* 1997, Tilman 1999, Hooper and Vitousek 1997, Zak *et al.* 2003a, Spehn *et al.* 2005, Jonsson 2006, Lanta and Leps 2006), but these studies have often reached different conclusions about the contribution that species diversity itself make to ecosystem functioning. Interpretation of the experiments on the relationship between species and ecosystem processes has been controversial (Loreau *et al.* 2002). Most of these studies were undertaken under controlled conditions where species diversity in the experimental design was manipulated by altering either their composition or abundance or both.

The present study though is an attempt in the same direction, but differ significantly in its approach since it has been carried out in an undisturbed humid subtropical forest ecosystem characterized by high tree diversity showing highly uneven distribution pattern in the community. The relationship between tree diversity and N and P dynamics on the forest floor was investigated in the permanent plots dominated by different tree species by collecting data on production and decay of litter and fine roots, soil microbial biomass dynamics and nutrient mineralization. The following specific aspects were studied at monthly/ seasonal intervals, to achieve the objective:

1. Tree species composition and their phytosociological attributes,
2. Microclimatic condition and physico-chemical properties including N and P status of soil,
3. Accumulation, production and decomposition of tree litter,
4. Accumulation, production and decomposition of fine roots,
5. N and P input, accumulation and release through litter and fine roots and
6. N and P mineralization and soil microbial biomass C, N and P dynamics.

2

Review of Literature

In recent years study of relationship between biodiversity and ecosystem functioning has emerged as a major ecological issue. With the rate of species extinction rapidly increasing, there has been growing interest in determining how the loss of biodiversity might alter the rates of ecological processes that are vital to the functioning of ecosystems. Results of the study carried out by Cardinale *et al.* (2000) suggest that there may not be single, generalizable relationship between species diversity and ecosystem functioning because the relative contributions of different species to ecosystem functioning changes with time and space. The relationship between species diversity and ecosystem function needs to be investigated at a variety of spatial and temporal scales (Lacroix and Abbadie 1998, Aubert *et al.* 2004). The earliest empirical contributions to the field of biodiversity and ecosystem function were published in the middle of the 1990's (Tilman and Downing 1994, Naeem *et al.* 1994, 1995, 1996). These studies concluded that biodiversity mattered for ecosystem functioning. The study by Naeem *et al.* (1994, 1995, 1996) was performed in the Ecotron on artificial ecosystems comprised of several trophic levels (i.e. primary producers, consumers and predators) containing low, medium, or high biodiversity. Biodiversity was found to significantly affect several ecosystem processes (net primary productivity, rates of energy and nutrient fluxes); some processes increased with increase in biodiversity while others decreased. Tilman and Downing (1994) performed their study on grassland ecosystem at Cedar Creek, Minnesota. In their study, they used experimental treatments containing one to 24 species, and found that both productivity and retention of soil nutrients increased with plant diversity. Lamont (1995) tested the effect of ecosystem composition on its functioning. Diversity has been observed to either increase or decrease ecosystem productivity or stability. Henry *et al.* (1999) found that plant species richness along productivity gradients may be strongly influenced by total stem density, and differences in competitive ability among species do not necessarily create dramatic changes in species richness along fertility gradients. He *et al.* (2002) reported that the variation in total biomass with species richness was greater at high nutrient level than at low nutrient level, and found a positive relationship between species richness and productivity only at high nutrient level. Hughes and Roughgarden (2000) investigated the relationship between species diversity and stability of community biomass in the face of perturbations in species abundances.

There are very few models that incorporate biological complexity as a regulating component of ecosystem function. Spehn *et al.* (2005) presented a multisite analysis of the relationship between plant diversity and ecosystem functioning within the European BIODEPTH (BIODiversity and Ecological Processes in Terrestrial Herbaceous ecosystems) network of plant diversity manipulation experiments. They reported that against geographical variation, all aspects of plant diversity and composition (i.e. both numbers and types of species and functional groups) produced significant positive impacts on ecosystem processes.

Lanta and Leps (2006) manipulated species and functional group richness of species assemblages composed of 16 species from four functional groups (grasses, legumes, creeping non legume forbs, and rosette non legume forbs) to evaluate the productivity- diversity relationship in a green house pot experiment. There was a pronounced increase in average aboveground biomass and a mild increase in belowground biomass with biodiversity. The effect of functional group richness was more pronounced than the effect of the number of species. Many researchers consider ecosystem processes to be more consistently associated with functional composition (presence of certain plant functional types or traits) and/or functional richness (number of different plant functional types) than with the species richness itself (Grime 1997, Hooper and Vitousek 1998, Diaz and Cabido 2001).

Most studies, however, have used particular species or random species compositions from smaller species pools, thus not being able to draw conclusions regarding effects of biodiversity per se. Instead, the results may be relevant only to the species used in the study. The persistence of biodiversity effects observed in controlled, short-term experiments has been questioned (Symstad *et al.* 2003). Since most studies to date have been performed over relatively short periods, it is not well known if they are relevant to effects of biodiversity in natural systems. However, in a long-term, grassland study it was found that the initial effect of biodiversity persisted over time although the underlying mechanisms changed (Tilman *et al.* 2001). In a plant diversity experiment without legumes for four consecutive years, a positive relationship between plant species richness and productivity emerged in the second year and strengthened with time (Van Ruijven and Brendse 2005). Nutrient analysis revealed that complementarity in nutrient uptake and nutrient use efficiency at high species richness are the two important underlying mechanism of diversity effects on ecosystem functioning.

The problem with most studies so far is that, while natural systems often are highly complex, experimental set–ups have used relatively few species and trophic levels. Studies using low complexity often have obtained quite straightforward results, but results from more complex experimental systems have been difficult to interpret. Thus, there is a trade-off between complexity and interpretability of results, and there are still no good solutions to this problem although attempts to perform studies on complex systems are being made.

Few studies in natural forest ecosystems address the relationship between biodiversity and ecosystem functioning. In the study by Lugo (1992) the primary differences between the more species rich secondary forests and less species rich pine and mahogany plantations (both exotics in Puerto Rico) were in the allocation of carbon and rate of nutrient cycling. The plantations had higher aboveground biomass and net primary production than the forest, but had significantly lower belowground biomass and production. The different species composition contributed to different patterns in the allocation of resources and carbon cycling mechanisms, highlighting the fact that there are multiple possible combinations of species for the maintenance of ecosystem function. In a tropical pine plantation and broadleaf secondary forest, Cuevas *et al.* (1991) found that both ecosystems had approximately the same net primary production but the plantation allocated most of its production to aboveground parts (>90%), whereas the secondary forest allocated almost 50% to the belowground parts. The secondary forests cycled nitrogen, phosphorus and potassium rapidly through the plant-soil-atmosphere interfaces and were able to capture nutrients that became available through mineralization. The functional diversity in nutrient retention mechanisms was greater in the plantations, but the diversity of nutrient capture and transfer mechanisms were greater in the secondary forests. In total, although secondary forests had more species than the plantations, this did not appear to result in greater nutrient accumulation or net primary production. Wardle *et al.* (1997a) made extensive study of ecosystem properties on 50 relatively pristine forested islands of varied size and plant biodiversity. The ecosystem properties like higher microbial biomass, high litter quality, and more rapid rates of litter decomposition and nitrogen mineralization coincided with lower botanical diversity and earlier successional state of the vegetation on larger areas. Aubert *et al.* (2004) assessed the patterns of variation during stand development of the humic epipedon and vegetation diversity in a pure European beech (*Fagus sylvatica* L.) forest and in a mixed beech-hornbeam (*Carpinus betulus* L.) forest in Normandy, France and found that the presence of an early successional mull forming species (hornbeam) could reduce the negative impact of beech monoculture by improving decomposition processes and thereby diversity of herbaceous plant assemblages. Oostra *et al.* (2006) quantified the impact of tree species on soil C stocks and soil acidity in southern Sweden in a non replicated 67-year-old monocultures of ash (*Fraxinus excelsior* L.), beech (*Fagus silvatica* L.), elm (*Ulmus glabra* Huds.), hornbeam (*Carpinus betulus* L.), Norway spruce (*Picea abies* L.) and oak (*Quercus robur* L.). They interpreted the result that differences in soil pH and SOC was species impact, because of homogeneous site conditions and similar land use history.

Results of the study carried out by Chen (2006) on the relationship between tree diversity, carbon storage and soil nutrient in an old growth forest of mixed broad leaved Korean pine forest, a typical vegetation type of China, suggest that the composition and evenness of dominant tree species at a small scale have great effects on carbon storage and nutrient content. It was found that at small scale, tree carbon storage generally increases with increasing tree species richness, but for stands with same species richness, tree carbon storage varies dramatically. Also, stands with similar tree composition at small scale have different soil organic storage and nutrient contents.

Grime (1997) emphasized that productivity and nutrient cycling are controlled by the biological characteristics of the dominant plants rather than their numbers. Hooper and Vitousek (1997), Loreau (2000) argued that ecosystem responses to plant richness could occur via complementary resource use if plant species differ in the way they take up nutrients, light and water either in space or in time. Not all species are equivalent in their control over the rates of ecological processes. Interspecific differences in resource use and efficiency can interact with uneven distribution of species abundance to result in one taxon or a select few taxa having disproportionate influence on a process. Wardle *et al.* (1998) made a comparative approach involving 20 dicotyledonous herbaceous species and concluded that there are clear linkages between plant ecophysiological traits, biotic interactions involving plants and ecosystem level properties and processes. Wardle *et al.* (2003) studied the response of soil food web to the identity and diversity of plant species and functional groups and found that plant species identity, not the diversity, may operate as an important driver of soil food webs, both at the levels of whole trophic group and within the trophic group. These results point to the importance of plant traits in driving the decomposer sub-system and indicate the potential value of a plant trait based approach for understanding how soil communities may respond to the composition of plant communities.

Evidences so far available suggest that trees of different species may generate significant differences in soils in the areas affected by their roots and litterfall, but whether these differences are important for regeneration, growth, species richness and productivity of tropical forests remains to be determined (Parker 1994).

In a classic study, Zinke (1962) showed that a single *Pinus contorta* tree growing in a sand dune along the coast of California modified the chemistry of the soil (pH, exchangeable cations and nitrogen) underneath its crown. Finzi *et al.* (1998a) have also reported that species generated soil heterogeneity has implications for stand level estimates of biogeochemical processes such as carbon storage and nitrogen cycling as well as has implications on plant diversity and regeneration. However, contrasting result was reported from species rich Costa Rica tropical rainforest by Powers *et al.* (2004) that although emergent tree species may affect soil chemical and nutrient availability, these effects cannot be generalized to all tree species.

Agricultural researchers generally have emphasized the role of initial C-to-N ratios in controlling decomposition and N mineralization (Smith and Sharpley 1990, Ranells and Wagger 1996), while forest scientists have highlighted lignin and lignin-to-N ratios as predictors for forest litter (Aber *et al.* 1990, Cotrufo *et al.* 1995, Cortez *et al.* 1996, Issac and Nair 2006). In tropical agricultural systems, polyphenols (PP) have also been found to be important predictors of mulch decay and N mineralization. Organic materials with high lignin and polyphenol (PP) contents, or high PP-to-N ratios or lignin + PP-to-N ratios, have low decomposition and N mineralization rates (Tian *et al.* 1992, Seneviratne *et al.* 1998, Seneviratne 2000). Berg and Ekbohm (1991) and Geng *et al.* (1993) have reported that water–soluble materials were the most or one of the most significant chemical variables affecting forest litter decay during the first year of the decomposition process.

Zimmer (2002) studied the influence of species richness on the decomposition of woodland leaf litter. He observed that overall leaf litter decomposition was high when low biotic activity was combined with high leaf litter species richness. He therefore concluded that species richness promotes decomposition of leaf litter and recycling of nutrients. Loranger *et al.* (2002) studied the influence of soil properties and litter quality on decomposition rate in two semi-evergreen tropical forests. These studies support the contention that litter quality is one of the important determinants of decomposition in tropical forest and differences in soil characteristics and fauna did not seem to be enough to affect decomposition. Madritch and Hunter (2004) reported that intraspecific litter diversity can influence some ecosystem functions in the presence of another species, but the overall chemical quality of litter is more important to nutrient fluxes during decomposition. Valenzuela-Solano and Crohn (2006) assessed the influence of chemical composition on the decomposition and N release rates from samples of 11 organic mulches enclosed in nylon mesh bags under field conditions at the University of California, Riverside and found that decomposition rates were largely determined by initial chemistry, but N release rates were dependent on both initial chemistry and behavior of the microorganisms that consumed them. Results of Prescott (1995) showed that N availability alone, either exogenous or endogenous (through fertilization or deposition) does not appear to control rates of litter decomposition in forests.

Reynolds and Hunter (2001) tested whether inputs from canopy herbivores would affect the critical soil processes of respiration, nutrient cycling and decomposition. They observed significant effects of litter exclusion, greenfall exclusion and throughfall additions on soil respiration.

Hansen (1999) found that increased decomposition of litter coincided with changes in the mite community suggesting *Quercus rubra* litter encouraged soil biota that increased its decomposition rate. In contrast, results of Ayers *et al.* (2006) showed that litter from three tree species (*Fagus sylvatica, Acer pseudoplatanus* and *Picea sitchensis*) did not decompose faster in the presence of indigenous soil biota, providing no support for the notion that woodland plants encourage the development of soil communities that rapidly decompose their litter.

Gartner and Cardon (2004) reviewed emerging research on interactions among leaves of different species during decomposition. The overall indications are that interactions of litters from different species in ecosystems do affect decomposition rates of individual leaf types in mixes, the consequent nutrient availability to plants, and /or the decomposer community structure and activity. Thus the emerging patterns in the mixed litter decomposition literature have implications for relationship between biodiversity and ecosystem function (in this case, the function being decomposition), and for potential mechanisms through which invasive plant species could alter carbon and nutrient dynamics in ecosystems.

Giardina *et al.* (2001) used 16 months laboratory incubations of soil sampled from two subalpine forest type of the central Rocky Mountain to examine the effects of litter quality and soil clay content on C and net N mineralization rates. They found aspen litter had lower (C/N– 52–71; lignin/N– 26) than the pine litter (C/N- 82–111; lignin/N- 40–57), but pine soils released an average of 238 g C kg^{-1}soil C over 16 month compared with 103 g C kg^{-1}soil C for aspen soils. Higher microbial biomass (mg kg^{-1} soil C) under pine also indicated that pine soil C was of higher quality than aspen soil C. Net N mineralization rates did not relate to species or to soil C mineralization rates, and neither C nor N mineralization rates were related to soil clay content.

Sayer (2006) reviewed 152 years of litter manipulation experiments and showed that the effects of manipulating litter changes and interactions between the variables influenced by the accumulation of litter, intensified treatment effects or masked responses, make the interpretation of results difficult. By decreasing substrate availability and altering the microclimate, litter removal changed fungal species composition and diversity and led to a decline in populations of soil fauna. However, litter addition did not provoke a corresponding increase in the abundance or diversity of fungi or soil fauna. Wardle *et al.* (2006) concluded that litter mixing effects on the abundance and diversity of decomposer biota are likely to be of secondary and generally of minor significance when compared to the effects of litter species identity and composition.

Jackson *et al.* (1997) provided the first global estimates for fine root biomass, length, surface area, and nutrient contents and their distribution with depth in soil. These data help enhance hydrological models (where fine roots control water absorption by plants and affect groundwater and atmospheric fluxes), improve estimates of nitrogen cycling and are useful in assessing consequences of nitrogen loading, and developing biochemical modeling of nutrient uptake globally. Sundarapandian *et al.* (1999) observed changes in fine root biomass and net primary productivity due to conversion of evergreen and deciduous tropical forests into forestry plantations of Teak, Acacia, Albizia, and Rubber in Western Ghats, South India. The lower biomass and NPP in plantations ecosystems was attributed to species composition, low organic matter and soil fertility.

King *et al.* (2005) evaluated the effects of elevated atmospheric CO_2 and soil resource availability on production and chemistry, mycorrhizal colonization, and decomposition of fine roots in an early- and late successional tree species that are economically and ecologically important in north temperate forests. They concluded that root contributions to soil C cycling will mainly be influenced by fine root production and turnover responses to the changing environment rather than changes in root chemistry in trembling aspen and sugar maple ecosystems. Ostertag (2001) examined patterns of fine-root (<2 mm diameter) biomass, belowground net primary productivity, and root turnover rates over a 1-yr period using sequential soil coring and a decomposition experiment, at three sites along a forest chronosequence in the Hawaiian Islands. These results suggested that root dynamics differ dramatically between ecosystems low in N and P, even though each system is regarded as infertile. N availability had a smaller effect on root dynamics than did P availability, suggesting that the simple dichotomy between fertile and infertile sites that is often evoked to explain plant characteristics may not be justified. Yang *et al.* (2004b) studied fine root (< 2 mm in diameter) distribution, seasonal pattern and net production during 1999–2001 in 33 year–old plantations of two coniferous trees, Chinese fir (*Cunninghamia lanceolata*) and *Fokienia hodginsii* and two broadleaved trees, *Ormosia xylocarpa* and *Castanopsis kawakamii*, and compared the results with that of an adjacent natural forest of *Castanopsis kawakamii* (~150 year old) in Sanming, Fujian, China. Conversion of native forest to tree plantations has reduced fine root biomass in the soil profile, especially in the uppermost 10 cm soil layer. Also, a decrease in fine root productivity and turnover, coupled with the decrease in aboveground litter production due to forest transformation, have important implications on consequences for C sequestration (lower SOM content), nutrient availability, and long–term site productivity. Yang *et al.* (2004c) showed that the decomposition of fine roots of *Cunninghamia lanceolata* and *Tsoongiodendron odorum* was controlled by chemical composition and found a change in TNC (total non-structural carbohydrates) - regulating the initial decomposition phase to lignin- or N- regulating in the second phase, and P or lignin- regulating in the last phase.

Effect of tree species on soil microbial biomass has also been studied, with concentrations of microbial C and N being lower in forest floor beneath conifers than beneath deciduous tree species (Bauhas *et al.* 1998). Menyailo *et al.* (2003) studied the soil microbial activities in tree based cropping systems and natural forests of the Brazilian Amazon and concluded that individual tree species of natural and secondary forests and species used in tree based crop plantations strongly affect N transformations in soil particularly net nitrification than C respiration. Loranger *et al.* (2006) found that changes in plant diversity and composition lead to a rapid response of bacterial activity and diversity in grassland ecosystems.

Soils of deciduous stands show higher N mineralization than soils of coniferous stands (Cot′e *et al.* 2000), probably due to differences in foliage litter quality, as net N mineralization was found to decrease strongly with increasing lignin content and with increasing lignin to N ratio (Scott and Binkley 1997). A comparable pattern has been found for net nitrification rates, i.e. high rates under deciduous species and low or no detectable rates under coniferous tree stands (Ste-Marie and Par′e 1999). Perez *et al.* (1998) also observed that field N mineralization rates were two times higher in a mixed-angiosperm (*Nothofagus nitida*) forest than in conifer-dominated (*Fritzroya cupressoides*) forest, and correlated it with greater N input via litterfall, higher soil pH and narrower C/N ratios of soils and litter in the former.

Zak *et al.* (2003a) provided evidence from a long term field manipulation of plant diversity (treatments containing 1–16 species) that soil microbial communities and key ecosystem processes that they mediate, are significantly altered by plant species richness. Microbial community biomass, respiration and fungal abundance significantly increased with greater plant diversity as did N mineralization rates. They concluded that the response of soil microbial communities could be an integral component of plant diversity's influence on ecosystem function. Dijkstra *et al.* (2005) studied the response of soil C and N dynamics to changes in atmospheric CO_2 (ambient, 560 ppm), N fertilization (0, 4 g N m^{-2} yr^{-1}), plant species number (1, 4 species), and plant functional group number (1, 4 groups; all with 4 species) in a grassland field experiment in Minnesotá, USA. Elevated CO_2, N fertilization, and increased plant diversity all increased plant productivity but these treatments differed significantly in their effects on C and N dynamics in the soil i.e. they have divergent effects on decomposition of rapid- and slow-cycling soil organic matter pools, microbial biomass, and net N mineralization rates that are potentially important in altering long-term soil C and N storage. Smolander and Kitunen (2002) compared soil microbial biomass and activities in different types of forest stands dominated by pure single-species of silver birch (*Betula pendula*), coniferous stands of Norway spruce (*Picea abies*) and Scots pine (*Pinus sylvestris*) mixed with birch. They reported that soil microbial biomass C and N, rates of C mineralization and net N mineralization as well as concentrations of DOC and DON were all highest in the silver birch stand or at least at the same level as in the coniferous stands. Templer *et al.* (2003) examined the effect of five tree species (*Fagus grandifolia, Tsuga Canadensis, Quercus rubra, Acer saccharum* and *Betula alleghanensis*) on soil microbial biomass nitrogen (MBN) and N transformations in soils of the Catskills Mountains, New York, USA. The results suggested that MBN and N transformations varied widely among the tree species but the patterns observed cannot be explained by differences in organic matter, C:N or soil moisture content. These variations among tree species might also have resulted forest N retention and loss. Brüggemann *et al.* (2005) studied the effects of five different tree species common in the temperate zone, i.e. beech (*Fagus sylvatica* L.), pedunculate oak (*Quercus robur* L.), Norway spruce (*Picea abies* [L.] Karst), Japanese larch (*Larix leptolepis* [Sichold and Zucc.] Gordon) and mountain pine (*Pinus mugo* Turra), on soil respiration, gross N mineralization and gross nitrification rates. They demonstrated that the significant differences in C and N turnover between the different tree stands were indeed affected by different tree species. Ralte *et al.* (2005) reported that human activities such as shifting agriculture and horticultural practices coupled with high rainfall in the hilly buffer zone of the Nokrek biosphere reserve cause depletion of the MBC and MBN, and reduction in dehydrogenase and urease activities in soil.

Knops *et al.* (2002) supports the view that plant species can have large impacts on ecosystem nitrogen cycling. The role of microbial decomposers in nitrogen cycling is much more important than that of the plants, but microbes are dependent on plants for carbon. Microbes control the nitrogen cycling, but plants regulate carbon inputs that control microbial activity. Thus, plant quality controls nitrogen cycling not because of a direct impact on nitrogen mineralization, but because plant carbon controls microbial immobilization. Lovett *et al.* (2004) investigated the influence of individual tree species on nitrogen (N) cycling in small single-species plots of five dominant tree species (*Acer Saccharum, Fagus grandifolia, Betula alleghaniensis, Tsuga canadensis* and *Quercus rubra*) in the Catskill Mountains of New York State and indicated that tree species can exert a strong control on N cycling in forest ecosystems that appears to be mediated through the quality of soil organic matter, but that standard measures of litter quality cannot explain the mechanism of control.

Finzi *et al.* (1998a) found interspecific differences in net N mineralization and forest floor C and N pools beneath beech (*Fagus grandifolia* Ehrh.), eastern hemlock (*Tsuga canadensis* Carr.), sugar maple (*Acer saccharum* Marsh.), red maple (*Acer rubrum* L.), white ash (*Fraxinus americana* L.) and northern red oak (*Quercus rubra* L.).

Menyailo *et al.* (2002) examined the effects of the six most commonly dominant tree species in Siberian forests

(Scots pine, spruce, Arolla pine, larch, aspen and birch) after 30 years of planting on soil C and N mineralization, N_2O reduction and N_2O production during denitrification. The six tree species studied were separated into three groups according to their effects on net N mineralization, net nitrification and denitrification. Thus, tree species caused significant changes in soil N transformations by modifying the amount and quality of soil organic matter and soil pH. Ehrenfeld *et al.* (2001) found increased soil pH and nitrification in stands invaded by two exotic species, *Berberis thunbergii*, a woody shrub and *Microstegium vimineum*, a C_4 grass which often co–occur, in three locations in northern New Jersey (USA). Thus, suggested that a variety of characteristics of the exotic species caused soil based ecosystem processes to change following invasion. The findings of Carney and Matson (2006) provide evidence for human alteration of soil microbial communities via alteration of the plant community composition and diversity and that such change are mediated in part by changes in soil carbon quality.

Several aspects of the humid subtropical forest ecosystems of Meghalaya have been studied by earlier workers. Khan and Tripathi (1989) reported the role of interactive influence of light intensity and soil moisture in the regeneration of *Alnus nepalensis* Don., *Quercus griffithi* Hk. and *Schima khasiana* Dyer. Microenvironmental variability and species diversity in tree fall gaps and forest under storey were studied by Barik *et al.* (1992). Barik *et al.* (1996) studied the effect of disturbance on natural regeneration of *Schima khasiana, Lithocarpus dealbatus* and *Quercus griffithii.* The effect of disturbance on the regeneration behaviour of *Casearia vareca* Roxb., *Eurya japonica* Thunb., *Psychotria symplicifolia* Kurz., and *Rhododendron arboreum* Sm of a sacred grove has been reported by Mishra *et al.* (2003).

Plant diversity and community characteristics of sacred groves of the Jaintia Hills were investigated by Jamir and

Pandey (2003) and Upadhya *et al.* (2003).They reported high species diversity and low dominance in all the groves. Mishra *et al.* (2004) studied the effects of anthropogenic disturbance on plant diversity and community structure of Swer sacred grove in East Khasi Hills of Meghalaya.

Arunachalam *et al.* (1996a) studied the decomposition dynamics of fine roots and N and P mineralization pattern during forest regrowth. Seasonal dynamics of microbial biomass C, N and P in 7–, 13– and 16–year old regrowth of a disturbed subtropical humid forest were studied by Maithani *et al.* (1996). Relationship between N-mineralization and quality of the litter was studied by Maithani *et al.* (1998). John *et al.* (2002) studied decomposition of fine roots of *Pinus kesiya* and turnover of organic matter, N and P of coarse and fine pine roots and herbaceous roots and rhizomes in sub tropical pine forest stands of different stages. Upadhaya *et al.* (2005) studied the dynamics of fine and coarse roots and nitrogen mineralization in a humid subtropical forest ecosystem and found that fine root growth and N mineralization was synchronized in a manner that helps in conservation of nitrogen in the soil.

Above review of literature, reveals that so far no study has been undertaken to assess the role of tree diversity on community level ecological processes such as litter decomposition, soil microbial biomass dynamics and nutrient mineralization in the humid subtropical forest ecosystem in northeast India in particular and other ecosystems found in rest of the country.

3

Study Site and Experimental Design

Location

The present study was carried out at Swer (Latitude $25^0 25.01'$ N and Longitude $91^0 47.47'$ E), a humid subtropical forest in East Khasi Hills district of Meghalaya, north-east India. The forest is well protected in the form of a sacred grove due to religious belief of the people.

The Swer sacred grove is about 32 km south of Shillong on the way to Cherrapunjee and covers an area of 12 ha. Its altitude varies between 1910 and 1975 m a.s.l. The topography of the forest varies from gentle east facing side slope (30^0) to very steep slope (55^0) to a cliff on the western side.

Climate

The climate of the area is monsoonic with distinct warm-wet season and cold-dry season. The rainy season starts from May and continues till October and more than 80% of the rain occurs during this period. The cold - dry period extends from November till March. The annual rainfall was about

10,754 mm and mean temperature was 23.5 °C during the study period.

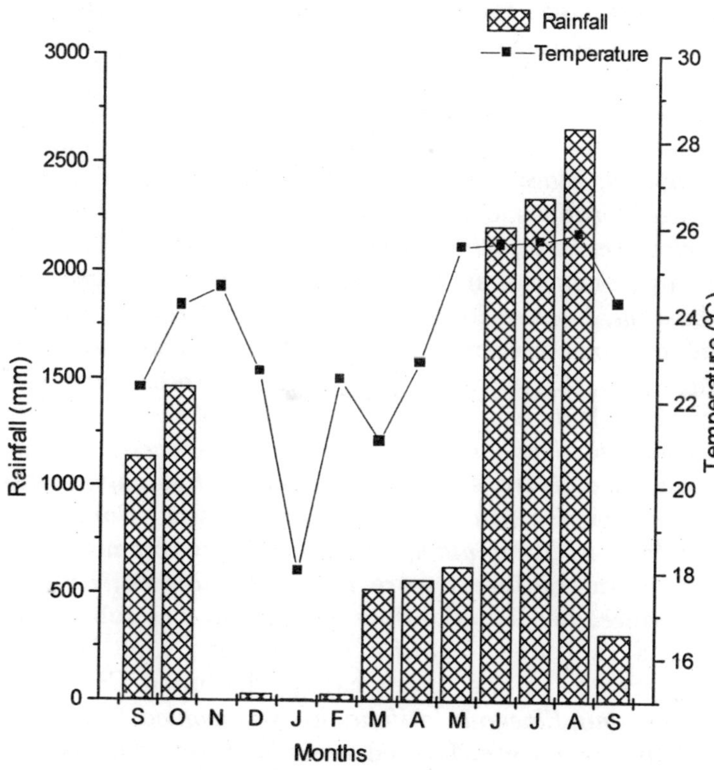

Figure 3.2 Mean monthly rainfall (mm) and temperature (°C) at Cherrapunjee during the study period (September 2004 to September 2005).

Vegetation

According to Champion and Seth (1968), the climax vegetation of the area is subtropical wet hill forest. Since majority of the tree species in the canopy and sub canopy layers are evergreen, the vegetation at Swer may be termed as subtropical evergreen forest. It is a closed canopy forest characterized by high tree diversity, complex community organization and high spatial heterogeneity in species distribution and forest microenvironment. The common evergreen trees found in the forest are *Rhododendron arboreum, Myrica esculenta, Symplocos javanica, Neolitsea cassia, Persea odoratissima, Magnolia pterocarpa,* etc. The deciduous elements included *Engelhardtia spicata, Ficus nerifolia* etc. The canopy is composed of *Cinnamommum bejolghota, Elaeocarpus lancifolius, Engelhardtia spicata, Persea odoratissima, Magnolia pterocarpa, Neolitsea cassia, Myrica esculenta, Rhododendron arboreum,* etc. The sub–canopy tree species are *Glochidion acuminatum, Ligustrum robustum, Lindera latifolia, Photinia integrifolia,* etc. The under canopy tree species includes *Lyonia ovalifolia, Eurya acuminata, Psychotria symplicifolia, Symplocos laurina* etc. The shrub layer was very thick composed of *Eurya japonica, Jasminum dispermum, Daphne papyracea, Daphne involucrata, Ixora subsessilis, Tupidanthus calyptratus, Viburnum foetidum, Smilax myrtillus, Corylopsis himalayana, Gleichinia* sp. etc. Some of the common lianas present in the forest were *Derris ferruginea, Embelia subcoriacea* and *Tupidanthus calyptratus.* The sub–canopy shrubs included *Daphne involucrata* and *Myrsine semiserrata.* In the under canopy included *Corylopsis himalayana, Elaegnus latifolia, Eurya japonica, Gaultheria fragrantissima* etc. formed a shrub layer. The ground vegetation was sparse and dominated by *Ophiopogon intermedius, Oplismenus burmannii, Balanophora diocia,* etc. Ferns and *Selaginella* were common on the forest floor. The tree trunks and branches were covered with profuse growth of mosses, ferns and epiphytes. Woody climbers and twiners were also abundant in the forest.

The tree density of the forest was 1328 trees ha^{-1} and basal area was 27.34 $m^2 ha^{-1}$. Based on IVI, the dominant tree species were *Rhododendron arboreum, Symplocos javanica, Magnolia pterocarpa, Persea gamblei, Myrica esculenta, Neolitsea cassia, Persea odoratissima, Photinia integrifolia.* The density and basal area of shrubs were 5296 individual ha^{-1} and 16.04 $m^2 ha^{-1}$ respectively.

Experimental Design

The forest under study was surveyed and patches differing distinctly in tree species composition were demarcated. The permanent experimental plots (10m×10m) dominated by *Myrica esculenta, Rhododendron arboreum* and *Neolitsea cassia* and by a number of other species (*Elaeocarpus lancifolius, Magnolia pterocarpa, Persea odoratissima* etc.) were laid within the forest. Three replicates of each of the above four types of experimental plots were identified in the forest and demarcated for the study.

Species composition and phyto-sociological attributes

IVI of trees, shrubs and herbs of the forest as well as those present in the permanent experimental plots were determined by methods outlined by Misra (1968) and Muller Dombois and Ellenberg (1974).

Table 3.1

Composition, density (per 300m^2) and basal area (m^2 per 300m^2) of tree species in the experimental plots

Experimental Plots	*Name of species*	*Density*	*Basal area (m^2)*
Myrica esculenta	*Myrica esculenta* Buch.–Ham.ex.D. Don.	14	3.257
	Rhododendron arboreum Sm.	13	0.543
	Symplocos javanica Kurz.	2	0.022
	Ficus nerifolia Sm.	1	0.014
	Eurya acuminata DC.	1	0.011
	Dendropanax japonicum Seem.	1	0.018
	Photinia integrifolia Lindl.	1	0.003
	Viburnum simonsii Hk. f. & Th.	1	0.003
	Total	34	3.87

(Contd...)

Experimental Plots	*Name of species*	*Density*	*Basal area (m^2)*
Rhododendron arboreum	*Rhododendron arboreum* Sm.	25	2.809
	Lyonia ovalifolia Drude.	2	0.215
	Persea odoratissima Koster.	1	0.02
	Eurya acuminata DC.	3	0.044
	Photinia integrifolia Lindl.	7	0.30
	Symplocos sp.	4	0.10
	Ficus nerifolia Sm.	1	0.02
	Symplocos javanica Kurz.	16	0.07
	Myrica esculenta Buch.–Ham.ex.D.Don.	3	0.08
	Engelhardtia spicata Leschm.ex.Bl.	1	0.02
	Total	63	3.67
Neolitsea cassia	*Neolitsea cassia* Koster.	13	1.603
	Prunus jenkinsii Hk.f.	1	0.019
	Persea odoratissima Koster.	2	0.086
	Psychotria symplicifolia Kurz.	1	0.003
	Derris sp.	1	0.004
	Liana	1	0.005
	Elaeocarpus acuminatus Wall.ex.Mast.	3	0.185
	Glochidion acuminatum Muell.–Arg.	2	0.009
	Total	24	1.91
Mixed	*Elaeocarpus lancifolius* Roxb.	4	1.449
	Persea odoratissima Koster.	4	0.218
	Glochidion acuminatum Muell.–Arg.	6	0.101
	Syzygium tetragonum Kurz.	3	0.109
	Derris sp.	3	0.036
	Liana	1	0.003
	Magnolia pterocarpa Roxb.	5	2.21
	Psychotria symplicifolia Kurz.	2	0.011
	Schefflera hypoleuca Harms.	1	0.007
	Tupidanthus calyptratus Hk.f.&Th.	1	0.01
	Total	30	4.15

Table 3.2
Shrubs present in experimental plots

Name of species	*Myrica plots*	*Rhododendron plots*	*Neolitsea plots*	*Mixed plots*
Jasminum dispermum Wall.	–	+	+	–
Melastoma malabathricum Linn.	+	+	–	–
Daphne papyracea Wall.ex Steud.	–	+	+	+
Eurya japonica Thunb.	+	+	–	–
Symplocos glomerata King ex Cl.	–	+	+	–
Lygodium sp	–	+	–	–
Smilax myrtillus DC	+	+	–	+
Lasianthus biermanii King ex Hk. f.	+	–	–	–
Ixora subsessilis G Don.	–	+	+	+
Corylopsis himalayana Griff.	+	+	–	–
Gaultheria fragrantissima Wall.	+	+	–	–
Tupidanthus calyptratus Hk .f. &Th.	–	+	+	+
Viburnum foetidum Wall.	+	+	–	–
Gleichinia sp.	+	+	–	–
Zanthoxylum oxyphylum Edgew.	–	–	+	+
Hedera helix Cl.	–	+	+	–

Table 3.3
Herbs present in experimental plots

Name of species	*Myrica plots*	*Rhododendron plots*	*Neolitsea plots*	*Mixed plots*
Anoectochilus roxburghii Lindl.	–	+	–	+
Oplismenus burmanii P.Beauv	+	+	–	–
Ophiopogon intermedius D.Don	+	+	–	+
Impatiens acuminata Benth. ex Hk.f. & Th.	+	+	–	–
Balanophora dioica Brown	–	+	+	+
Selaginella sp.	–	+	+	–

Table 3.4
Mean density, basal area and canopy cover of tree species in the experimental plots (each value is a mean of 3 replicates)

Experimental plots	*Density (no. of individuals 300 m^{-2})*	*Basal area (m^2)*	*Canopy cover (%)*
Myrica	11 (5)	1.29 (1.08)	73 (62)
Rhododendron	21 (8)	1.22 (0.94)	79 (51)
Neolitsea	8 (6)	1.07 (0.93)	81 (76)
Mixed	10	1.38	81

Values of the dominant tree species are indicated in the parentheses

In *Myrica* dominated plots, *Rhododendron arboreum, Symplocos javanica, Ficus nerifolia, Eurya acuminata, Dendropanax japonicum, Photinia integrifolia* and *Viburnum simonsii* were also present in small numbers. Shrubs in these plots included *Melastoma malabathricum, Smilax myrtillus, Lasianthus biermanii, Corylopsis himalayana* etc. Herb layer was very sparse and composed of *Oplismenus burmanii, Ophiopogon intermedius* etc. In these plots *M. esculenta* alone contributed 41% of the total tree density and 84% of the total basal area. The mean canopy cover of tree species in the experimental plots was 73%, of which 62% was contributed by *M. esculenta* (Table 3. 4).

Similarly, in *Rhododendron* plots, the associated tree species were *Symplocos javanica, Photinia integrifolia, Symplocos* sp. etc. The shrub layer was composed of *Daphne papyracea, Symplocos glomerata, Ixora subsessilis, Hedera helix, Gleichinia* sp. etc. Few of the herbaceous species encountered in the plots includes *Anoetochilus roxburghii, Oplismenus burmanii, Ophiopogon intermedius,* and *Balanophora dioica, R. arboreum* represented 40% of the total tree density and 77% of the total basal area. The mean canopy cover of tree species was 79%, of which 51% was that of *R. arboreum* alone.

In *Neolitsea* plots, however, trees of *Elaeocarpus acuminatus, Glochidion acuminatum* and *Persea odoratissima* were also present. *Psychotria symplicifolia, Ixora subsessilis, Tupidanthus calyptratus* and *Hedera helix* were the dominant shrubs and *Selaginella* sp. and *Balanophora dioica* were dominant among the herbaceous species. *N. cassia* contributed 54% to the total tree density, 84% to the tree total basal area and 76% to the tree canopy cover.

The dominant tree species in the mixed plots were *Elaeocarpus lancifolius, Glochidion acuminatum, Persea odoratissima* and *Magnolia pterocarpa. Ixora subsessilis, Tupidanthus calyptratus* and *Daphne papyracea* were the dominant shrubs while *Balanophora dioica* and *Anoetochilus roxburghii* were the dominant herbs. The mean density of tree species was 10 individuals per 100 m^2. Basal area was 1.38 m^2 per 100 m^2 and canopy cover was 81%.

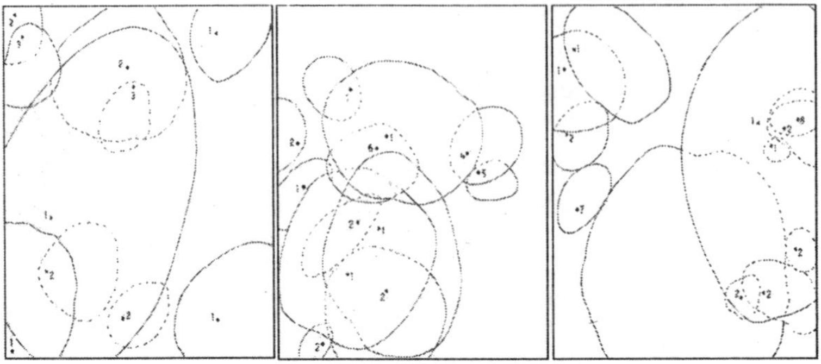

Figure 3.3 Distribution and canopy cover of tree species in *Myrica esculenta* plots

1. *Myrica esculenta* (14), 2. *Rhododendron arboreum* (13), 3. *Symplocos javanica* (2), 4. *Ficus nerifolia* (1), 5. *Eurya acuminata* (1), 6. *Dendropanax japonicum* (1), 7. *Photinia integrifolia* (1) and 8. *Viburnum simonsii* (1)

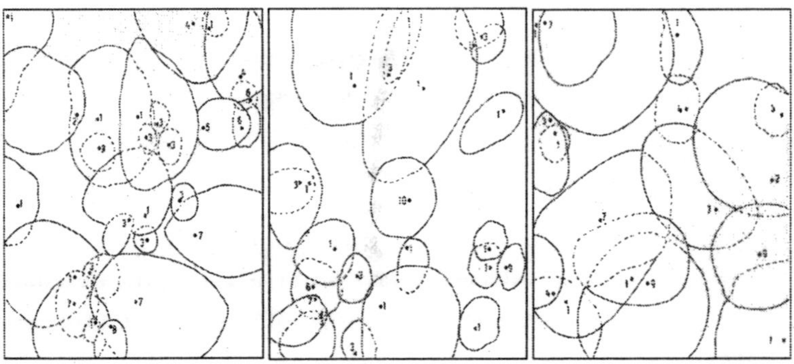

Figure 3.4 Distribution and canopy cover of tree species in *Rhododendron arboreum* plots

1. *Rhododendron arboreum* (25), 2. *Lyonia ovalifolia* (2), 3. *Persea odoratissima* (1), 4. *Eurya acuminata* (3), 5. *Photinia integrifolia* (7), 6. *Symplocos* sp. (4), 7. *Ficus nerifolia* (1), 8. *Symplocos javanica* (16), 9. *Myrica esculenta* (3) and 10. *Engelhardtia spicata* (1)

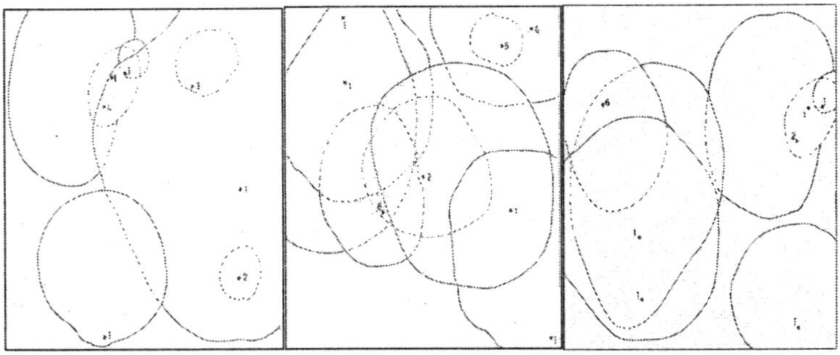

Figure 3.5 Distribution and canopy cover of tree species in *Neolitsea cassia* plots

1. *Neolitsea cassia* (13), 2. *Prunus jenkinsii* (1), 3. *Persea odoratissima* (2), 4. *Psychotria symplicifolia* (1), 5. *Elaeocarpus acuminatus* (3) and 6. *Glochidion acuminatum* (2)

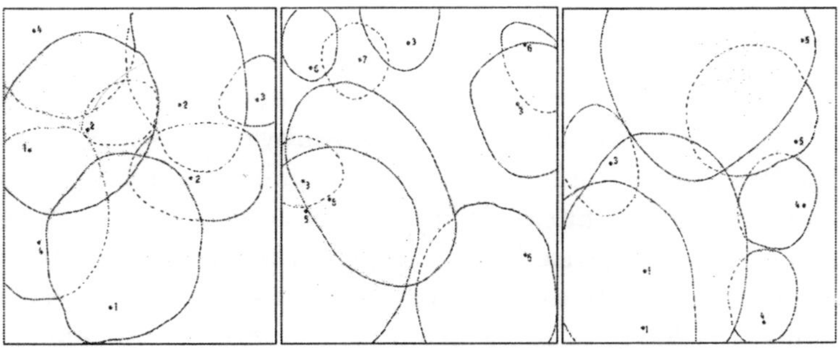

Figure 3.6 Distribution and canopy cover of tree species in Mixed plots

1. *Elaeocarpus acuminatus* (4), 2. *Persea odoratissima* (4), 3. *Glochidion acuminatum* (6), 4. *Syzygium tetragonum* (3), 5. *Magnolia pterocarpa* (5), 6. *Psychotria symplicifolia* (2) and 7. *Schefflera hypoleuca* (1)

4

Forest Microclimate and Soil Physico-Chemical Properties

Introduction

The forest vegetation produces a complex 3–dimensional mosaic of microclimate varying vertically from canopy top to the forest floor and horizontally from point to point beneath the canopy (Richards 1996).The microclimate could be considered the 'pulse' of an ecosystem because of its direct and indirect effects on most ecosystem processes and vice versa (Xu *et al.* 2004). It is the result of the interactions among various biological, biophysical, hydrological and topographical factors in an ecosystem. The microclimate determines the conditions for productivity and activities of the soil organisms (Martius *et al.* 2004).

Vegetation type, community structure and canopy closure influence the microclimate on the forest floor (Martius *et al.* 2004, Upadhaya 2002, Raich and Tufekciouglu 2000). Tree stands modify the microclimate (Brüggemann *et al.* 2005) in terms of reduced air and surface soil temperature, increased relative humidity and reduced irradiance compared to grasslands (Dela Cruz and Luna 1994, Luna *et al.* 1999).

Vegetation is one of the primary factors controlling soil genesis (Jenny 1980). The relationship between soil nutrient status and availability and plant diversity is very complex in forest. Tree species differ significantly in their influence on soil properties, biogeochemical cycles as well as soil fertility (Augusto *et al.* 2002). Individual trees also influence the substrates upon which they grow and may leave their imprints on the soil by their crown and roots. Zinke (1962) showed that a single *Pinus contorta* tree growing on a sand dune along the coast of California modified the chemistry of the soil underneath its crown. The supply of nitrogen typically differs under the influence of different species on the same soil type; the rates of trace gas fluxes (including NO, N_20 and CH_4) may also differ. The influence of global changes on soils and feedback between soils and the atmosphere will depend more strongly on changes in the distribution of tree species across landscapes, than on the direct effects of climate on soils (Binkley and Menyailo 2005).

Tree species growing on a uniform parent material (Boettcher and Klinsz 1990, Oostra *et al.* 2006) can influence the size and distribution of nutrient pools across soil horizons (Berendse 1998, Binkley 1992) through soil solution uptake, root production and turnover, mycorrhizal activity, organic compound exudation and quantity and quality of litter produced for decomposition (Binkley and Giardina 1998). Species generates soil heterogeneity that has implications for stand level estimates of biogeochemical processes such as carbon storage and nitrogen cycling and influence plant diversity and regeneration (Finzi 1998a).

Experiments conducted so far have demonstrated positive effects of plant diversity on phosphorus (Naeem *et al.* 1995), nitrate (Ewel *et al.* 1991, Naeem *et al.* 1995, Tilman *et al.* 1996), ammonium (Tilman *et al.* 1996), and total nitrogen (Hooper and Vitousek 1997, Naeem *et al.* 1995). Contrary to the results of these workers inconsistent or no effect of plant diversity on total nitrogen (Hooper and Vitousek 1997, Naeem *et al.* 1995), nitrate nitrogen (Naeem *et al.* 1995), ammonium nitrogen (Ewel *et al.* 1991, Naeem *et al.* 1995) and phosphorus (Ewel *et al.* 1991, Hooper and Vitousek 1997) have been reported.

Temporal variation in forest microclimate and soil physical and chemical properties in the (upper layer 0–10 cm) of the four permanent experimental plots have been presented in this chapter to examine the influence of tree diversity on these attributes of the community.

Methods

Measurements of forest microclimate

The microclimatic condition (light intensity, air temperature, and relative humidity) was measured close to the forest floor at several points in each experimental plot at monthly intervals. Light intensity was measured by Digital Luxmeter (TES 1332A), air temperature and relative humidity by Thermo hygrometer TH–103 (Mex–therm). Soil temperature was measured using a digital soil thermometer (Multi-thermometer).

Soil sampling

Soil samples were collected at monthly interval for one annual cycle during September 2004 to September 2005 from the permanent plots. Three replicate samples were collected for the surface layer (0–10 cm depth) from each plot using a steel corer (10 cm diameter). The replicated samples were mixed thoroughly to obtain one composite sample. Fresh samples were used for the analysis of soil moisture content and soil pH and the rest were air-dried and sieved through 2 mm sieve and stored for further analysis.

Soil analysis

Soil texture was determined by Bouyoucos hydrometer

method. Bulk density was estimated by gravimetric method (Allen *et al.* 1974) and porosity was calculated using bulk density data. Water holding capacity (WHC) was determined by Keen's box method by using copper cups of 5.6 cm internal diameter and 1.6 cm height (Piper 1942). Soil moisture content was determined by taking 10 g fresh sieved soil (Allen *et al.* 1974). A digital pH meter (SYSTRONICS–335) was used to determine pH in 1:2.5 w/v suspension of soil in deionized water (Anderson and Ingram 1993).

Organic carbon was determined by colorimetric method (Anderson and Ingram 1993). Soil organic matter content was obtained by multiplying the soil organic carbon content by 1.724 assuming that the SOM contains 58% of carbon (Allen *et al.* 1974). Total Kjeldahl nitrogen was determined by Kjeldahl digestion distillation method (Allen *et al.* 1974). Available phosphorus was determined after extracting soil phosphorus in 0.5 M sodium bicarbonate solution by ammonium-molybdate blue method (Allen *et al.* 1974).

Statistical analysis

The data was analysed using two-way ANOVA to test the effect of months/seasons and tree species on microclimatic variables and physico-chemical properties of the soil. Fisher LSD test was carried out to compare the mean values. Correlation analysis was carried according to Zar (1974).

Results

Forest Microclimate

Light intensity and air temperature were found to be significantly high in *Myrica* plot (Figure 4.1 and 4.3), compared to other plots. There was no significant variation ($p<0.01$) in light intensity between *Rhododendron, Neolitsea* and Mixed plots (Table 4.2). There was a drastic reduction in light intensity from *Myrica* to the Mixed plot (59–99%) as compared to open (Figure 4.2). Significant difference ($p<0.05$)

was observed across the months with high intensity during winter and spring and low during rainy season (Table 4.1). Variation ($p<0.001$) in air temperature between *Rhododendron* and *Neolitsea* plots, and between *Neolitsea* and Mixed plots was not significant (Table 4.2). However, a gradual reduction in air temperature was observed from *Myrica* to the Mixed plots (Figure 4.4). Relative humidity, on the other hand, showed a reverse trend to that of light intensity and air temperature with high percentage in *Neolitsea* and Mixed plots (80%) and low in *Myrica* plots (67%) (Figure 4.5). It varied significantly ($p<0.001$) across the months with high value during rainy and low during winter (Table 4.1).

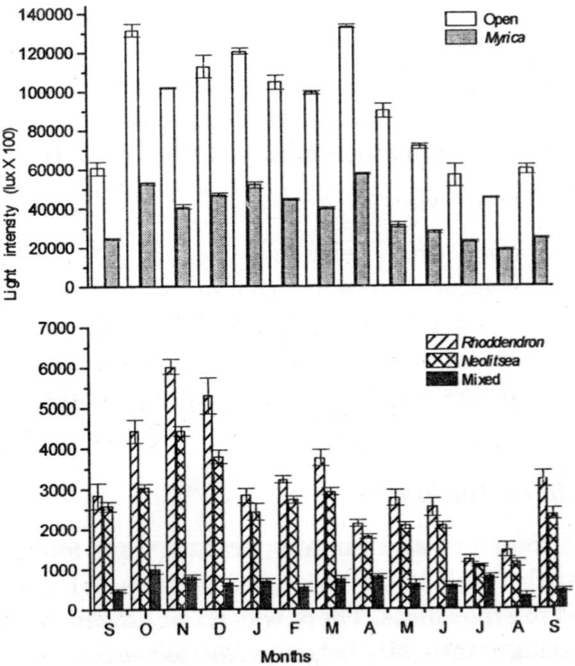

Figure 4.1 Monthly variations in light intensity in open and in different experimental plots

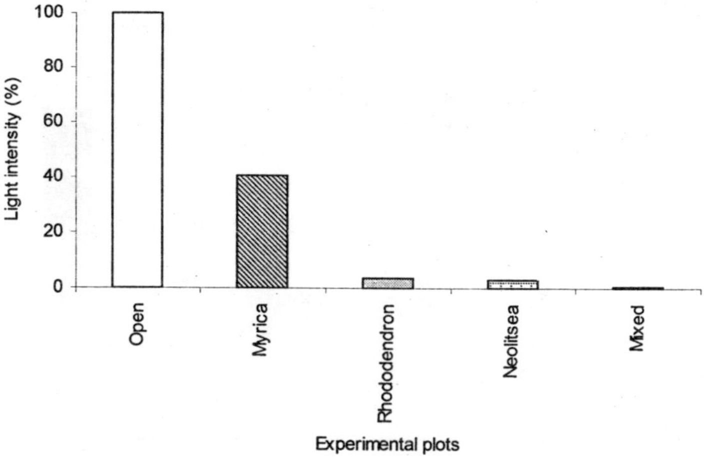

Figure 4.2 Relative average percent reductions in light intensity in different experimental plots in relation to open areas outside the forest

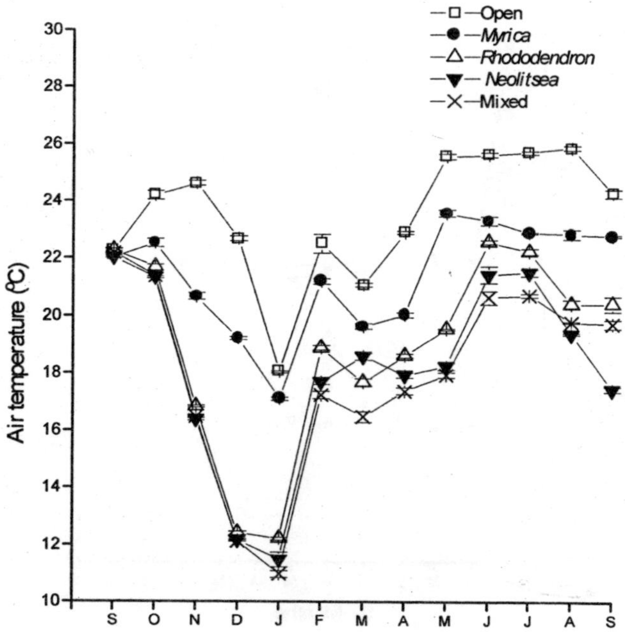

Figure 4.3 Monthly variations in air temperature in different experimental plots and outside the forest in open

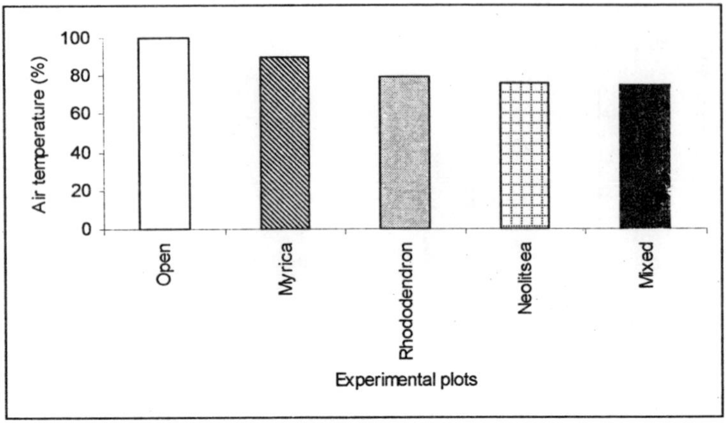

Figure 4.4 Relative average percent reductions in air temperature in different experimental plots in relation to open area outside the forest

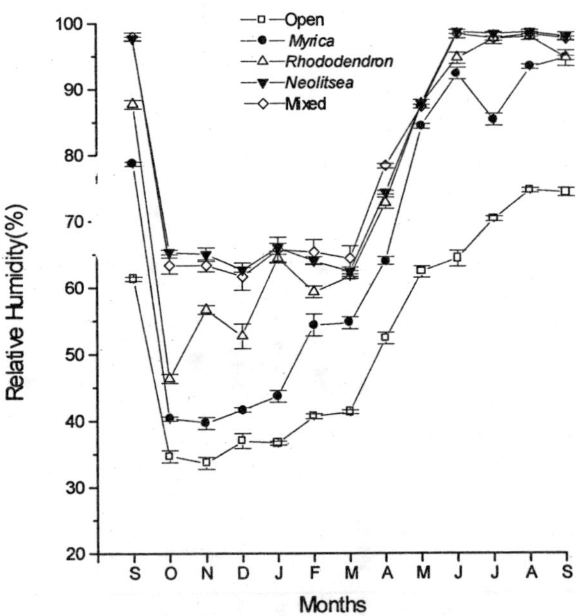

Figure 4.5 Monthly variations in relative humidity in different experimental plots and in open area outside the forest

Table 4.1

Two way ANOVA showing effects of months and experimental plots on light intensity (Lux), air temperature (^0C) and relative humidity (%)

Parameters	*Source of variation*	*Degrees of freedom*	*Calculated F value*	*Tabulated F value*	*Significance level (P)*
Light Intensity	Months	12	2.38	1.9	<0.05
	Plots	4	108.57	3.7	<0.01
Air Temperature	Months	12	49.20	2.7	<0.001
	Plots	4	120.93	4.6	<0.001
Relative Humidity	Months	12	309.35	2.7	<0.001
	Plots	4	339.72	4.6	<0.001

Table 4.2

Mean light intensity (Lux), air temperature (^0C) and relative humidity (%) in different experimental plots (each value is a mean of 39 measurements taken between September 2004 and September 2005)

Experimental plots	*Light intensity*	*Air temperature*	*Relative humidity*
Open	91,426	23.79	52.59
Myrica	37,213	21.36	66.69
Rhododendron	3,215[a,b]	18.90[d]	74.92
Neolitsea	2,495[a,c]	18.01[d,e]	79.90[g]
Mixed	656[b,c]	17.92[e]	79.95[g]
LSD	7,885	0.84	2.29
Significance level	<0.01	<0.001	<0.001

[a,b,c] Values with similar superscripts a, b, c are not significantly different at p<0.01

[d,e,f,g] Values with similar superscripts d, e, f, g are not significantly different at p<0.001

Soil Physical Properties

Soil texture, Bulk density and Water holding capacity

Soil texture ranged from Loamy sand in *Myrica* plot to Sandy loam in the other three plots. Clay content (12.88%) was low in *Myrica* plots but other three plots did not differ significantly in this respect. Bulk density ranged from 0.84 - 0.86 g cm^{-3} and did not vary significantly between the experimental plots. Water holding capacity ranged from 60-62% in the plots without significant variation between them. It was highest in *Rhododendron* plot (62.29%) and lowest in *Myrica* plot (60.30%) (Table 4.3).

Soil temperature

Two way ANOVA revealed significant variation ($p<0.001$) in soil temperature across the months and plots (Table 4.7). It was in order of *Myrica* > *Rhododendron* > *Neolitsea* ≥ Mixed plot (Table 4.8). In all the experimental plots, the soil temperature was low during winter and high during rainy season (Figure 4.6).

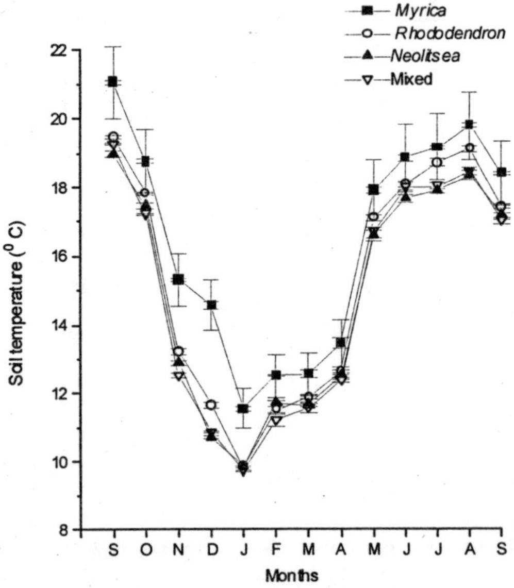

Figure 4.6 Monthly variations in soil temperature in the experimental plots

Table 4.3

Proportion of soil particles (%), textural class, bulk density (BD, g cm^{-3}), porosity (%) and water holding capacity (WHC, %) in different experimental plots

Experimental plots	*Clay (%)*	*Silt (%)*	*Sand (%)*	*Textural Class*	*BD (g cm^{-3})*	*Porosity (%)*	*WHC (%)*
Myrica	12.88 ±1.53	20.64 ±2.41	66.48 ±0.96	Loamy sand	0.84 ±0.01	68.30 ±0.33	60.30 ±0.10
Rhododendron	16.57 ±0.37	21.72 ±0.24	61.71 ±0.60	Sandy loam	0.86 ±0.04	67.55 ±1.36	62.29 ±0.17
Neolitsea	16.17 ±0.58	22.75 ±0.45	61.08 ±1.03	Sandy loam	0.85 ±0.01	67.92 ±0.50	60.81 ±0.03
Mixed	16.73 ±1.12	21.44 ±2.69	61.83 ±3.74	Sandy loam	0.85 ±0.01	67.83 ±0.45	60.98 ±1.19

Soil moisture content

Among the experimental plots, the mean soil moisture ranged from 36% to 45% and it did not vary significantly between *Rhododendron, Neolitsea* and Mixed plots. *Myrica* plot recorded the lowest soil moisture content (36.49%) (Table 4.8). The variation across the months was highly significant ($p<0.001$) (Table 4.7). It ranged from 40 – 57% during rainy to 23 – 35% during winter season (Figure 4.7).

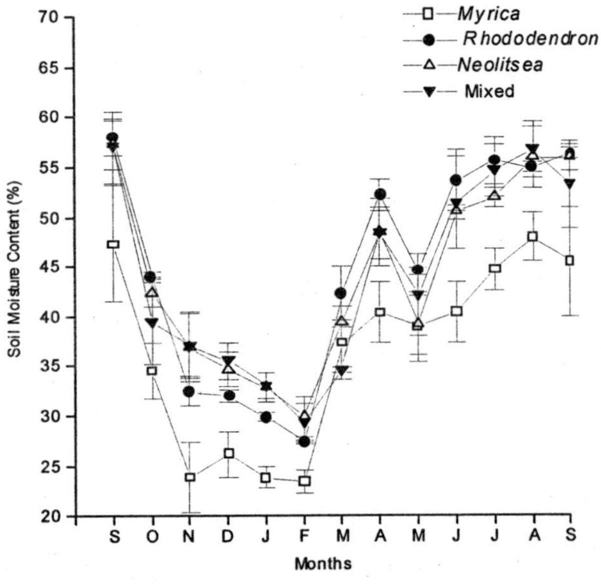

Figure 4.7 Monthly variations in soil moisture content in the experimental plots

Soil Chemical Properties

Soil pH

The soil was acidic in nature with pH range of 4.36 – 4.64. Among the experimental plots, the *Myrica* plot was more acidic (pH 4.36) as compared to the other three plots; pH was high in the Mixed plot (pH 4.60). However, the values were similar in *Rhododendron* and *Neolitsea* plots. It showed marked seasonality with high values during winter and low during rainy season (Figure 4.8).

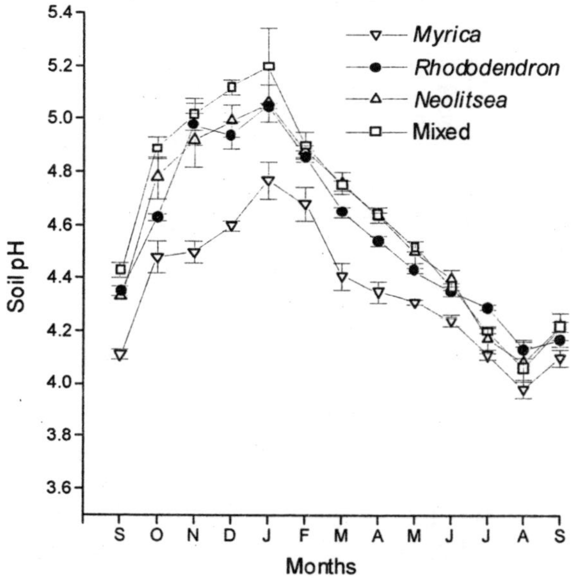

Figure 4.8 Monthly variations in soil pH in different experimental plots

Soil organic carbon and organic matter

Soil organic carbon (SOC %) and organic matter (SOM %) varied significantly ($p<0.001$) across the seasons (Table 4.7). The values were high during winter in *Neolitsea* and Mixed plots and during spring in *Myrica* and *Rhododendron* plots and low during rainy season in all the plots (Table 4.4). Amongst the plots, highest SOC was in *Rhododendron* plot (3.11%) followed by Mixed (2.88%) and *Neolitsea* plot (2.84%) and the lowest was recorded in the *Myrica* plot (2.69%). Variation between *Rhododendron* and other three plots was significant ($p<0.001$). But *Myrica, Neolitsea* and Mixed plots had similar SOC content. However, in SOM content, significant variation was observed amongst all the experimental plots (Table 4.8).

Table 4.4

Seasonal variation in soil organic carbon content (SOC, %) and soil organic matter content (SOM, %) in different experimental plots

Experimental plots	*Autumn*		*Winter*		*Spring*		*Rainy*		*Autumn*	
	SOC (%)	*SOM (%)*	*SOC (%)*	*SOM (%)*	*SOC (%)*	*SOM (%)*	*SOC (%)*	*SOM (%)*	*SOC (%)*	*SOM (%)*
Myrica	2.66 ± 0.18	4.58± 0.31	2.85 ± 0.40	4.92± 0.68	2.94 ± 0.42	5.06 ± 0.73	2.28 ± 0.02	3.93 ± 0.04	2.72 ± 0.23	4.69 ± 0.40
Rhododendron	3.06 ± 0.08	5.27 ± 0.14	3.34 ± 0.11	5.76 ± 0.19	3.48 ± 0.18	5.99 ± 0.32	2.68 ± 0.06	4.62 ± 0.10	2.99 ± 0.10	5.15 ± 0.17
Neolitsea	3.04 ± 0.13	4.89 ± 0.06	3.07 ± 0.08	5.29 ± 0.25	3.04 ± 0.02	5.14 ± 0.12	2.58 ± 0.03	4.32 ± 0.24	2.69 ± 0.20	5.02 ± 0.16
Mixed	2.82 ± 0.19	4.86 ± 0.34	3.08 ± 0.11	5.32 ± 0.19	3.07 ± 0.31	5.30 ± 0.54	2.69 ± 0.10	4.63 ± 0.17	2.74 ± 0.05	4.72 ± 0.09

Total Kjeldahl Nitrogen

Total Kjeldahl nitrogen (TKN %) in soil also varied significantly ($p<0.001$) across the season and experimental plots (Tables 4.7 and 4.8) with higher concentration during winter season and low during rainy season (Table 4.5). Among the experimental plots TKN was high in Mixed plots (0.89%) followed by *Neolitsea* plots (0.82%), *Rhododendron* plots (0.79%) and lowest in *Myrica* plots (0.59%).

Table 4.5
Seasonal variation in total Kjeldahl nitrogen (TKN, %) in soils of the experimental plots

Experimental Plots	*Autumn*	*Winter*	*Spring*	*Rainy*	*Autumn*
Myrica	0.53 ±0.04	0.63 ±0.10	0.81 ±0.10	0.45 ±0.05	0.52 ±0.03
Rhodo-dendron	0.78 ±0.02	0.83±0.04	0.79 ±0.03	0.76 ±0.05	0.80 ±0.04
Neolitsea	0.72 ±0.09	0.92 ±0.07	0.85 ±0.05	0.78 ±0.07	0.80±0.07
Mixed	0.61±0.07	1.12±0.10	0.96±0.03	0.82±0.09	0.94±0.01

Available Phosphorus

Available P in soil also varied significantly ($p<0.001$) across the season (Table 4.7). High values were recorded during spring season and low during rainy season (Table 4.6). Among the experimental plots, it ranged from 2.57 – 5.16μg g^{-1} with higher values in *Neolitsea* plots (5.16μg g^{-1}) and lowest in *Myrica* plots (2.57μg g^{-1}). However, Mixed (4.07μg g^{-1}) and *Rhododendron* plots (3.82μg g^{-1}) did not show significant variation (Table 4.8).

Table 4.6
Seasonal variation in soil available phosphorus ($\mu g\ g^{-1}$) in the experimental plots

Experimental Plots	*Autumn*	*Winter*	*Spring*	*Rainy*	*Autumn*
Myrica	2.98 ±0.60	2.11 ±0.37	3.30 ±0.58	1.77 ±0.19	2.66 ±0.21
Rhodo-dendron	4.51 ±0.01	2.93 ±0.26	4.71 ±0.01	2.32 ±0.05	4.62 ±0.01
Neolitsea	5.11 ±0.51	4.42 ±0.12	6.69 ±0.01	3.97 ±0.25	5.41 ±0.33
Mixed	4.04 ±0.28	3.79 ±0.34	5.15 ±0.43	2.72 ±0.29	4.67 ±0.19

Table 4.7
Two way ANOVA showing effects of months/seasons and experimental plots on temperature (^0C), moisture content (SMC %), pH, organic carbon (SOC %), organic matter (SOM %), total Kjeldahl nitrogen (TKN %) and available phosphorus (Av.P $\mu g\ g^{-1}$) in soils of the experimental plots

Parameters	*Source of variation*	*Degrees of freedom*	*F value*		*Significance level*
			Calculated	*Tabulated*	
Soil Temperature	Months	12	898.40	2.7	<0.001
	Plots	3	147.5	5.4	<0.001
SMC (%)	Months	12	184.79	2.7	<0.001
	Plots	3	97.72	5.4	<0.001
Soil pH	Months	12	327.99	2.7	<0.001
	Plots	3	169.78	5.4	<0.001
SOC (%)	Seasons	4	21.79	4.6	<0.001
	Plots	3	15.45	5.4	<0.001
SOM (%)	Seasons	4	21.84	4.6	<0.001
	Plots	3	15.49	5.4	<0.001
TKN (%)	Seasons	4	20.38	4.6	<0.001
	Plots	3	48.67	5.4	<0.001
Av.P ($\mu g\ g^{-1}$)	Seasons	4	86.29	4.6	<0.001
	Plots	3	149.36	5.4	<0.001

Table 4.8
Mean physico-chemical properties of soils of the experimental plots (each value is a mean of 45 replicates taken across five seasons)

Experimental plots	*Soil temperature*	*SMC (%)*	*pH*	*SOC (%)*	*SOM (%)*	*TKN (%)*	*Av. P* ($\mu g\ g^{-1}$)
Myrica	16.47	36.49	4.36	2.69[a]	4.64	0.59	2.57
Rhododendron	15.28	44.81[a,b]	4.57[a]	3.11	5.36	0.79	3.82[a]
Neolitsea	14.89[a]	44.23[a,c]	4.59[a]	2.84[a,b]	4.90	0.82	5.16
Mixed	14.85[a]	44.07[b,c]	4.64	2.88[b]	4.96	0.89	4.07[a]
LSD	0.23	1.46	0.035	0.16	0.28	0.07	0.32
Significance level	<0.001	<0.001	<0.001	<0.001	<0.001	<0.001	<0.001

[a,b,c] Values with similar superscript alphabets a,b,c in the rows are not significantly different at $p<0.001$.

Discussion

Analysis of microclimatic data in the experimental plots revealed that light intensity near the forest floor changed with the change in species composition and canopy cover, from *Myrica* to Mixed plots. It reduced drastically in *Myrica* plot (59%), *Rhododendron* plot (96%), *Neolitsea* plot (97%) and Mixed plot (99%) as compared to the open area outside the forest. Air temperature also reduced in the similar fashion. Contrary to this, relative humidity increased from *Myrica* to Mixed plots. Gradual increase in canopy cover from *Myrica* plots (73%), to *Rhododendron* plots (79%), *Neolitsea* and Mixed plots (81%) was responsible for such a change in light intensity and air temperature in the forest understorey. Rijkers *et al.* (2000) also reported a significant positive relationship between direct measurements of photon flux density and percentage canopy openness in French Guiana rain forest. The *Neolitsea* and Mixed plots were similar in microclimatic condition due to presence of more common species and closeness between the two types of plots. The present findings are in conformity with those of Dela Cruz and Luna (1994), Luna *et al.* (1999), Raich and Tufekciouglu (2000), Rijkers *et al.* (2000), Upadhaya (2002), Martius *et al.* (2004) and Brüggemann *et al.* (2005). Species-specific differences in tree architecture also strongly influence microclimate. Differences in leaf size, their display and phenology, as well as branch size and bifurcation frequency can alter pathways of light penetration and air movement within the crown affecting temperature, humidity and photosynthetic light availability (Meinzer and Goldstein 1996).

Effect of canopy openness on the soil temperature under *Myrica* plots, was more apparent than the other plots. The stronger effect of canopy opening on soil temperature found in *Myrica* plots than in other three plots may be attributed to greater input of radiant energy owing to the location of plots near the forest periphery. The close correlation between soil temperature and radiant energy input at the soil surface was reported in a study by Balisky and Burton (1993). The amount of precipitation reaching the forest floor depends on the canopy morphology of the tree species. Greater radiant energy in *Myrica* plots was responsible for the lower soil moisture content due to high evaporation and low water retention due to high proportion of sand. Greater soil moisture content in *Rhododendron* plots on the other hand was primarily due to greater accumulation of litter on the forest floor (Chapter 5) and SOM that check evaporation losses and helps in moisture retention in the soil.

Soil bulk density is a sensitive indicator of compaction and is also an important index of soil quality (Acosta-Martinez *et al.* 1999). In the present study, bulk density followed the order: *Myrica* < *Neolitsea* < Mixed < *Rhododendron*, though the differences between them were not significant ($p>0.05$).

Marginal decrease in bulk density could be attributed to the changes in the percentage of sand and clay (Guerrero *et al.* 2000) and SOM content. A small decrease in WHC from *Rhododendron* to *Myrica* plots is attributed to increase in proportion of sand particles and decrease in organic matter content in the later plots.

The data also clearly show that tree species had an effect on soil chemical properties. Though the soil was acidic in all plots, but it was more acidic in *Myrica* plot than the other three plots. Lower soil pH in *Myrica* plots could be due to the relatively thick litter layer and slower rates of litter decomposition (discussed in Chapter 5). This finding is consistent with the studies of Konova (1966) and Finzi *et al.* (1998b) suggesting that relatively thick forest floor litter and slower rates of decomposition increases the quantity of organic acids thereby lowers the soil pH. The acidic reaction of the soil is due to presence of exchangeable Al^{+3} and intensive leaching of bases, therefore, a drop in the pH during rainy season could be the result of excessive leaching of basic cations by rain water (Wild 1996).

Differences in soil characteristics under different tree species with homogeneous site condition and similar land use history have been reported from temperate forests (Brüggemann *et al.* 2005, Finzi *et al.* 1998a, 1998b, Boettcher and Kalisz 1990), monoculture plantation (Oostra *et al.* 2006, Rhoades 1997, Fisher 1995), tropical forests (Rhoades *et al.* 1994), and mixed fir plantation in China (Huang *et al.* 2005). Rawat (2005) found that tree species affect soil characteristics such as pH, soil organic carbon, available phosphorus and potassium in montane forest of Garhwal Himalayas. Chavan *et al.* (1995) have also reported that forest tree species in the 10-year-old plantation at forestry block of Central Experimental Station, Wakawali (Maharashtra) did not change the physical properties of the soil under the canopy, but the effect on the chemical properties such as organic carbon, nitrogen, phosphorus and potassium was conspicuous. Carney and Matson (2006) also reported that soil characteristics such as moisture content, extractable nitrate, organic carbon, nitrogen and pH varied significantly with plant diversity, monoculture type and three species combination from Costa Rica. However, Powers *et al.* (2004) have reported contradictory result from species rich Costa Rica rain forest that emergent tree species may affect soil chemical and nutrient availability but these effects cannot be generalized to all tree species.

Highest SOM content in *Rhododendron* plots could be attributed to greater litter and fine root accumulation. High concentration of TKN and Av. P in Mixed and *Neolitsea* plots respectively could be due to greater nutrient return through litter and fine roots as discussed in Chapter 7. *Myrica* plots had lowest SOM, TKN and Av. P content. Similar results were obtained by Dudley *et al.* (1996) from coastal heathland ecosystem. They reported that nitrogen fixed by *Myrica pensylvanica* did not add to the soil nitrogen pool. Leaching of from the soil because of sandy nature of soils could be one of the reasons for low N status in the soil. Dutta and Agrawal (2002) also reported that plots with *Cassia siamea* (N-fixing species) showed lowest N content in the soil compared with other non N-fixing plants due to poor nodulation. Walker (1993) did not find any correlation between the presence of N-fixing species and total N accumulation in surface soil.

5

Litter Dynamics

Introduction

In forest ecosystems, majority of net primary production returns to the soil surface as plant litter and subsequently enters the decomposition pathway (Swift *et al.* 1979). Litter production and decomposition rates have great importance in maintaining fertility of the soil. The integrity of the ecosystem is maintained by the nutrients returned to the soil as litterfall and its decomposition (Rajendraprasad *et al.* 2000). The quantity of litterfall varies greatly over a range of spatial and temporal scales and is determined mainly by climate, seasonality, topography, site quality, and species composition (Haase 1999, Sundarapandian and Swamy 1999, Norgrove and Hauser 2000, Yang *et al.* 2004a, 2005). Management practices can cause drastic changes in litter production by modifying species composition and productivity; climate change may affect litterfall as changes in rainfall patterns and mean annual temperatures can affect tree phenology and tree species distribution (Condit *et al.* 1996). An increase in productivity and litterfall has been observed as a consequence of elevated atmospheric CO_2 levels (DeLucia *et al.* 1999, Allen *et al.* 2000, Finzi *et al.* 2001, Schlesinger and Lichter 2001, Zak *et al.* 2003b).

The decomposition subsystem mineralizes the plant litter and is responsible for the replenishment of the pool of plant available nutrients, thereby maintaining ecosystem productivity (Swift *et al.* 1979). A thorough understanding of plant litter decomposition is indispensable for better understanding of the functioning of terrestrial ecosystems. The rates of decomposition show considerable spatial variation due to change in canopy architecture and tree species. The most important factors that affect litter decomposition are temperature, humidity and aeration which affect soil biota activity and litter composition and its quality. Within an ecosystem, plant litter quality is the main determinant of litter decomposition rate (Aerts 1997). Plant species may differ widely in quality and quantity of the litter they produce. Decomposition and subsequent mineralization of nutrients is therefore strongly determined by growth and decomposition characteristics of litter of the dominant plant species in an ecosystem. Organic matter deposition and decomposition rate may not be constant along the year and over the surface, thereby they contribute to the creation of different microhabitats on the forest floor. In natural forest, leaf litter usually consists of a mixture of a different species contributed annually. Blair *et al.* (1990) did not observe any difference between decomposition rates of single-species litter and mixed-species litter, but more recent comparative studies revealed that nutrient supply to the soil due to decomposition was enhanced when oak and beech litter was present in addition to pure pine litter (Conn and Dighton 2000). The findings suggest that besides the activity of saprophagous soil animals and saprotrophic microbiota, the species composition of the leaf litter influences its decomposition. Zimmer (2002) hypothesized that species richness promotes decomposition processes and thus nutrient recycling.

The amount of accumulated plant litter varies greatly in both space and time (Facelli and Pickett 1991). The heterogeneous nature of litter cover promotes species coexistence (Facelli and Pickett 1991) by facilitating or suppressing seed germination and seedling emergence, and by influencing seedling survival at a small scale in patches throughout the forest. As litter affects so many different variables simultaneously, it is difficult to quantify the consequences of changes in litter inputs at the ecosystem level.

In the present chapter, data related to annual accumulation, input and decay pattern of litter in the four permanent experimental plots are presented and attempt has been made to assess in the impact of tree diversity on these processes.

Methods

Forest floor litter mass

Amount of litter present in the experimental plots in the beginning and at the end of the study was determined by laying three (1m×1m) quadrats randomly on the forest floor in each of the permanent plots during September 2004 and September 2005 respectively.

Litterfall

Litterfall was measured on a monthly basis from September 2004 to September 2005 in all the permanent plots. Prior to the commencement of the sampling in the month of August 2004, 1m×1m permanent quadrats were laid randomly on the forest floor with the help of split bamboo stems to check litter loss by runoff water during rainy season. The litter present in each quadrat was collected and surface cleaved. Freshly fallen litter were collected from each quadrat at monthly interval and brought to the laboratory for separation and processing. Annual production is based on values recorded from October 2004 to September 2005.

Processing of different litter components

The litter samples (both forest floor litter and litterfall) were brought to the laboratory and were sorted into leaf litter of dominant tree species, mixed leaf litter, woody litter (<20mm in diameter) and miscellaneous litter (flowers, fruits, bark and other unidentified plant detritus). The separated samples were washed under a fine jet of water for removing the adhered soil particles. These were oven-dried at 80^{0}C for 48 hr and weighed. Samples of a given category of the litter were finely ground in a CYCLOTEC (Tecator) and stored for chemical analyses.

In situ leaf litter decomposition

In situ leaf litter decomposition was studied using nylon mesh (2 mm) litterbag (15cm×15cm) (Gilbert and Bocock 1960). Newly senesced leaves fallen on ground were collected from the permanent plots in June 2004. The collected leaf litters were air-dried in the laboratory. Ten grams of the air-dried leaves were placed in each bag and stitched with nylon threads. 40 bags each of leaf litter of dominant tree species and mixed leaf litter (including leaf litter of dominant tree species) were prepared and buried in surface soil layer (0–10 cm) during August, 2004 in their respective plots. Three litterbags were retrieved at monthly intervals. The litters were washed gently to remove the adhering soil particles and dried at 80°C for 48 hours and weighed.

Analysis of plant materials

The ash content was determined by igniting the sample at 550°C for 6 hours in a muffle furnace. Carbon content was calculated as 50% of the ash free weight. Nitrogen and phosphorus contents were determined according to Allen *et al.* (1974) and lignin was determined following the method outlined by Peach and Tracey (1956).

Litter turnover

Litter turnover rate (k_L) was calculated using mathematical model of Reiners and Reiners (1970)

$k_L = L / X_L$

where, L= annual litterfall (kg ha^{-1} yr^{-1}) and X_L= Mean annual standing crop (kg ha^{-1})

Turnover time (T) was calculated as a reciprocal of turnover rate

T= $1/k_L$, where, T= time in year.

Annual decomposition rate constant (k) was calculated using the negative exponential decay model (Olson 1963)

$k = (\ln (x/x_o))/t$

Where, x_o= initial dry weight; x= weight remaining at the end of the investigation and t is the time in years. The time required for 50 % (t_{50}) and 99% (t_{99}) decay were calculated as $t_{50} = 0.693/k$ and $t_{99} = 5/k$.

Statistical analysis

The data was analysed using two-way ANOVA to test the effect of months and tree species on litterfall, litter accumulation and weight loss. Fisher LSD test was carried out to compare the mean values. Correlation analysis was carried according to Zar (1974).

Results

Litterfall

The total annual litterfall ranged from 9,535 – 12,827 kg $ha^{-1}yr^{-1}$ with highest amount in *Rhododendron* plots (12,827 kg $ha^{-1}yr^{-1}$) followed in decreasing order by *Myrica* (11,732 kg $ha^{-1}yr^{-1}$) *Neolitsea* (11,393 kg $ha^{-1}yr^{-1}$) and Mixed plots (9,535 kg $ha^{-1}yr^{-1}$) (Table 5.5). The values were significantly different ($p<0.01$) between the plots. The leaf litter (leaf litter of dominant tree species and mixed leaf litter) constituted 71 – 84 percent of the total litterfall. Branches and miscellaneous materials accounted for 15 – 29 percent only. The leaf fraction of dominant species ranged from 6,299 kg $ha^{-1}yr^{-1}$ in

Neolitsea, to 6,902 kg $ha^{-1}yr^{-1}$ in *Myrica* and 7,293 kg $ha^{-1}yr^{-1}$ in *Rhododendron*. The seasonal pattern of litterfall in the experimental plots was similar for both the leaf and total litter.

In *Myrica, Rhododendron* and *Neolitsea* plots there were two distinct peaks one in March and another in August. In Mixed plots, only one distinct peak was observed in March (Figure 5.1).

Litter accumulation

Litter accumulation on the forest floor ranged from 4,334-6,147 kg ha^{-1}. It was highest in *Rhododendron* plots (6,147 kg ha^{-1}) and lowest in Mixed plots (4,334 kg ha^{-1}). Of the total litter accumulation, leaf litter (leaf litter of dominant tree species and mixed leaf litter) comprised 71 – 82 percent. The leaf fraction of dominant species ranged from 1,647 kg ha^{-1} in *Neolitsea* to 3,700 kg ha^{-1} in *Myrica* and 4,067 kg ha^{-1} in *Rhododendron*, accounting for 36 – 66 percent of the total litter accumulation.

The turnover rate varied from 2.04 yr^{-1} – 2.51 yr^{-1}. The plots may be arranged in the following order based on turnover rate: *Neolitsea* > Mixed > *Rhododendron* > *Myrica*. The turnover time varied from 0.41yr in *Neolitsea* to 0.49 yr in *Myrica* plot.

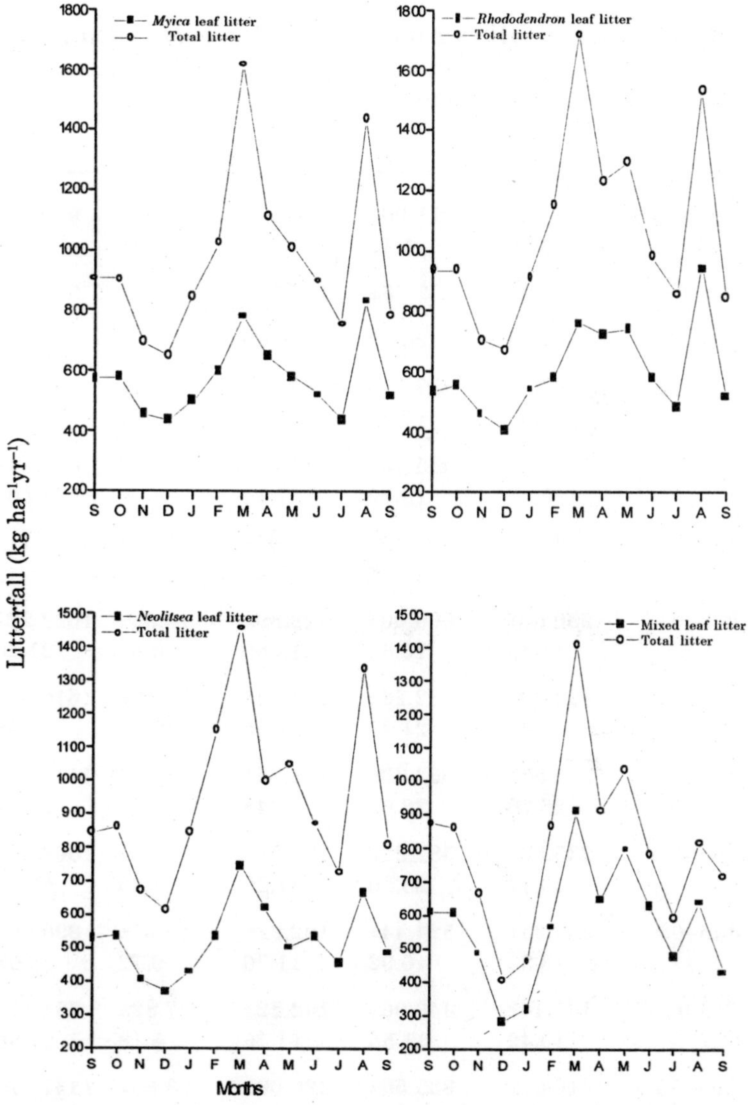

Figure 5.1 Monthly litterfall patterns of leaf litter of dominant tree species and total litter of the experimental plots

Table 5.1
Monthly litterfall (kg ha^{-1}) in *Myrica esculenta* plots

Months	*mixed leaf litter*	*leaf litter*	*woody*	*misc.*	*total*
Sep–04	204.00± 3.05	571.00± 1.15	124.00± 3.21	6.00± 3.46	905.00± 3.51
Oct–04	208.89± 17.36	577.78± 20.12	117.78± 9.69	–	904.45± 29.02
Nov–04	146.67± 11.55	457.78± 17.78	84.44± 10.42	6.67± 6.67	695.56± 28.02
Dec–04	126.67± 9.43	435.56± 18.19	91.11± 7.54	–	653.34± 20.82
Jan–05	222.22± 15.07	497.78± 26.76	120.00± 16.33	11.11± 11.11	851.11± 31.47
Feb–05	280.00± 11.55	600.00± 16.33	128.89± 18.59	13.33± 6.67	1022.22± 21.20
Mar–05	493.33± 17.64	782.22± 21.20	284.44± 21.55	56.89± 17.72	1616.88± 18.58
Apr–05	275.56± 26.20	653.33± 26.67	168.88± 26.48	15.78± 9.72	1113.55± 34.74
May–05	235.56± 30.14	582.22± 23.20	177.78± 21.20	13,33± 7.45	1008.89± 53.76
Jun–05	253.33± 13.33	524.44± 16.92	102.22± 11.76	16.67± 9.72	896.66± 25.93
Jul–05	164.44± 10.42	440.00± 11.55	142.22± 11.76	7.82± 5.18	754.48± 27.62
Aug–05	246.67± 28.28	835.56± 31.58	320.00± 13.33	28.89± 9.49	1431.12± 47.74
Sep–05	204.44± 12.37	515.56± 15.56	57.78± 7.03	5.56± 2.94	783.34± 23.57

Table 5.2
Monthly litterfall (kg ha^{-1}) in *Rhododendron arboreum* plots

Months	*mixed leaf litter*	*leaf litter*	*woody*	*misc.*	*total*
Sep–04	249.00± 7.03	534.67± 4.25	140.67± 10.17	11.67± 0.88	936.00± 4.35
Oct–04	240.00± 18.86	555.56± 12.37	137.78± 13.52	–	933.34± 24.04
Nov–04	160.00± 11.55	462.22± 20.12	64.44± 5.56	11.11± 5.88	697.77± 30.63
Dec–04	168.89± 11.11	404.44± 14.05	84.44± 8.01	12.22± 8.13	669.99± 23.45
Jan–05	231.11± 11.11	542.22± 25.04	140.00± 21.08	–	913.33± 22.61
Feb–05	417.78± 33.41	577.78± 25.04	155.56± 26.20	–	1151.12± 65.58
Mar–05	564.44± 14.05	760.00± 86.67	315.56± 18.19	80.00± 18.86	1720.00± 94.04
Apr–05	391.11± 31.11	724.44± 45.43	106.67± 20.00	9.78± 5.17	1232.00± 48.12
May–05	306.67± 21.08	742.22± 34.07	208.89± 20.85	32.22± 11.03	1290.00± 50.83
Jun–05	253.33± 9.43	577.77± 16.48	128.89± 11.11	18.89± 6.33	978.88± 24.18
Jul–05	213.33± 17.64	484.44± 18.19	137.78± 7.03	23.11± 8.08	858.66± 28.35
Aug–05	368.89± 19.75	942.22± 21.20	177.78± 15.07	40.00± 11.55	1528.89± 29.64
Sep–05	213.33± 13.33	502.00± 15.07	97.78± 11.76	15.56± 5.56	828.67± 18.29

Table 5.3

Monthly litterfall (kg ha^{-1}) in *Neolitsea cassia* plots

Months	*mixed leaf litter*	*leaf litter*	*woody*	*misc.*	*total*
Sep–04	198.67± 6.48	525.67± 12.34	115.33± 6.74	4.00± 4.00	843.67± 11.86
Oct–04	191.11± 8.89	537.78± 18.99	128.89± 16.02	–	857.78± 32.05
Nov–04	155.56± 10.42	404.44± 26.20	102.22± 7.03	11.11± 11.11	673.33 ± 27.08
Dec–04	137.78± 7.03	369.78± 42.58	104.44± 10.42	–	612.00± 43.79
Jan–05	266.67 ± 17.64	431.11± 40.84	151.11± 12.96	–	848.89± 46.92
Feb–05	351.11± 8.89	537.78± 35.97	248.89± 8.89	11.11± 5.88	1148.89± 45.35
Mar–05	488.89± 14.57	746.67± 22.11	217.78± 15.07	2.89± 2.89	1456.23± 24.28
Apr–05	240.00± 9.43	622.22± 34.71	137.77± 11.76	–	999.99± 33.30
May–05	302.22± 24.14	502.22± 25.04	208.89± 12.96	36.44± 10.82	1049.77± 33.53
Jun–05	244.44± 14.05	533.33± 13.33	93.33± 11.55	–	871.10± 24.75
Jul–05	146.67± 9.43	457.78± 22.22	97.78± 15.07	24.27± 12.89	726.50± 18.40
Aug–05	400.00± 13.33	666.67± 58.50	240.00± 23.09	28.89± 11.11	1335.56± 56.00
Sep–05	195.56± 10.42	488.89± 14.57	115.56± 14.05	13.33± 5.77	813.34± 26.46

Table 5.4
Monthly litterfall (kg ha^{-1}) in Mixed plots

Months	*leaf litter*	*woody*	*misc.*	*total*
Sep–04	610.66±12.14	246.00±4.04	15.67±8.00	872.33±1.76
Oct–04	608.89±16.02	253.33±14.91	–	862.22±17.78
Nov–04	488.89±16.02	168.89±8.89	8.89±5.88	666.67±16.33
Dec–04	284.44±20.49	109.78±13.25	14.44±9.88	408.66±35.22
Jan–05	320.00±16.33	136.44±13.56	8.00±8.00	464.44±14.44
Feb–05	568.89±23.83	275.56±19.37	22.67±9.18	867.11±31.54
Mar–05	911.11±31.11	448.89±36.38	51.11±23.36	1411.11±63.17
Apr–05	648.00±19.60	225.87±18.80	37.91±9.66	911.78±36.06
May–05	800.00±20.00	205.33±17.94	27.56±13.05	1032.89±31.30
Jun–05	631.11±33.18	137.78±11.76	11.78±8.81	780.67±26.69
Jul–05	475.55±15.56	109.56±10.29	10.58±5.63	595.68±15.79
Aug–05	640.00±24.94	153.78±20.74	23.56±6.27	817.34±19.43
Sep–05	431.11±24.75	253.33±36.51	31.78±14.02	716.22±52.92

Table 5.5
Mean annual accumulation (kg ha^{-1}), production (kg $ha^{1}yr^{-1}$), turnover rate (k, yr^{-1}) and turnover time (yr) of litter on the forest floor in different experimental plots

Experimental plots	*Litter fractions*	*Litter mass*	*Litter fall*	*Turnover rate (k,yr^{-1})*	*Turnover time (t, yr)*
1	*2*	*3*	*4*	*5*	*6*
Myrica	Leaf litter	3700± 193	6902	1.87	0.53
	Mixed leaf litter	1000± 166	2858	2.86	0.35
	Branches+ miscellaneous	1060± 203	1972	1.86	0.54
	Total	**5760± 77**	**11,732**	**2.04**	**0.49**

(Contd...)

1	2	3	4	5	6
Rhododendron	Leaf litter	4067± 196	7293	1.79	0.56
	Mixed leaf litter	820± 151	3529	4.30	0.23
	Branches+ miscellaneous	1260± 147	2006	1.59	0.63
	Total	**6147± 218**	**12,827**	**2.09**	**0.48**
Neolitsea	Leaf litter	1647± 235	6299	3.82	0.26
	Mixed leaf litter	1577± 112	3120	1.98	0.51
	Branches+ miscellaneous	1320± 62	1975	1.50	0.67
	Total	**4544± 217**	**11,393**	**2.51**	**0.40**
Mixed	Mixed leaf litter	3260± 210	6808	2.10	0.48
	Branches+ miscellaneous	1074± 183	2727	2.54	0.40
	Total	**4334± 220**	**9,535**	**2.20**	**0.45**

Initial chemical composition of leaf litter of dominant tree species

Carbon content in the leaf litter varied significantly from a minimum of 43.66% in *Neolitsea* to a maximum of 47.50% and 46.16% in *Myrica* and *Rhododendron* respectively. Nitrogen content varied significantly ($p<0.01$) between the species from a minimum of 0.90% in *Rhododendron* to a maximum of 1.57% in *Neolitsea.* Phosphorus content was low in all the leaf litter. It varied from a maximum of 0.065% in *Neolitsea* to a minimum of 0.04% in *Rhododendron.* C/N ratio varied widely from a minimum of 27.80 in *Neolitsea* to a maximum of 51.66 in *Rhododendron.*

Leaves of *Neolitsea* (22.14%) had low lignin content whereas, that of *Rhododendron* (35.36%) had high content (Table 5.6).

Initial chemical composition of mixed leaf litter

Carbon content in mixed leaf litter varied from 45.66%

to 48.33% with high values in *Myrica* plot as compared to the other three plots. Nitrogen content varied from 1.03% to 1.67% with high values (1.67%) in *Neolitsea* and 1.63% in Mixed plots and low (1.23%) in *Myrica* and 1.03% in *Rhododendron* plots. Phosphorus content varied from 0.032% to 0.067% with high concentration in *Neolitsea* and Mixed plots and low in *Myrica* plots. The C/N ratio was low in *Neolitsea* (27.44) and Mixed (28.12) plots and high in *Myrica* (39.70) and *Rhododendron* (45.05) plots.

Lignin content in mixed leaf litter varied significantly ($p<0.001$) from a minimum of 17.62% in *Neolitsea* to a maximum of 37.80% in *Rhododendron* plot (Table 5.6).

Litter decomposition

Leaf litter showed three distinct phases of decomposition (Figure 5.2). The first phase lasting for about 60 days was characterized by a rapid rate of decomposition (15 – 35% weight loss). This was followed by a period of slow weight loss lasting for another 200 days (7 – 15% weight loss). During the third phase i.e., between 270 and upto 400 days, decomposition was rapid (15 – 24% weight loss).

Rhododendron, Neolitsea and Mixed plots showed faster litter decomposition than *Myrica* plot. Most rapid decomposition of leaf litter occurred in *Neolitsea* (k= 0.89), followed by *Rhododendron* plots (k= 0.82), and *Myrica* (k= 0.53) (Figure 5.2). The time required for 50% decay (t_{50}) varied between the species and it increased from 0.78 in *Neolitsea* to 1.32 in *Myrica* leaf litter. Similarly, t_{99} also increased from 5.6 in *Neolitsea* to 9.52 in *Myrica* leaf litter (Table 5.7).

Decomposition of mixed leaf litter was most rapid in *Neolitsea* plots (k= 1.13) with 71% weight loss taking place during 400 days followed by *Rhododendron* (k= 0.98), Mixed (k= 0.85) and *Myrica* (k= 0.59) with 65%, 60% and 47% weight loss respectively taking place during the same period. The

Table 5.6

Initial chemical composition of leaf litter of dominant tree species and mixed leaf litter in the experimental plots. (± SE, n=3)

Parameters	*Myrica*		*Rhododendron*		*Neolitsea*		*Mixed*
	Leaf litter	*Mixed leaf litter**	*Leaf litter*	*Mixed leaf litter**	*Leaf litter*	*Mixed leaf litter**	*Mixed leaf litter*
C (%)	47.50±0.29	48.33±0.33	46.16±0.17	45.66±0.33	43.66±0.88	45.70±0.25	45.84±0.08
N (%)	1.27±0.06	1.23±0.10	0.90±0.05	1.03±0.10	1.57±0.03	1.67±0.02	1.63±0.04
P (%)	0.043±0.001	0.032±0.001	0.040±0.001	0.047±0.001	0.065±0.003	0.067±0.001	0.070±0.003
Lignin (%)	33.21±0.27	29.42±0.40	35.36±1.16	37.80±0.66	22.14±0.37	17.62±0.33	23.37±0.42
C/N	37.46±1.70	39.70±3.16	51.66±3.24	45.05±3.87	27.80±1.07	27.44±0.49	28.12±0.71
Lignin/N	26.20±1.22	24.16±1.86	39.41±1.14	37.23±2.89	14.08±0.31	10.58±0.34	14.44±0.64

*Includes leaf litter of dominant species in the respective plots

time required for 50% decay t_{50} also varied between the mixed leaf litters in different plots. It increased from 0.61 in *Neolitsea* to 1.18 in *Myrica* plots. Similarly, t_{99} also increased from 4.11 in *Neolitsea* to 8.53 in *Myrica* plots (Table 5.7).

The results showed a significant difference between the months and plots on weight loss pattern of leaf litter of dominant tree species ($p<0.05$; $F= 11.74$ and $F= 16.50$ respectively). Weight loss pattern of leaf litter was in the order of *Neolitsea* ≥*Rhododendron* ≥*Myrica* but the difference between them was not significant (Table 5.8). Significant effect of months and plots were also observed in case of mixed leaf litter ($p<0.05$; $F= 30.84$ and $F= 4.93$ respectively). The weight loss pattern of mixed leaf litter was similar to that exhibited by litters of dominant species (Table 5.8). In all the plots, significant ($p<0.05$) difference was observed between decomposition rate of single species leaf litter and mixed species leaf litter (Table 5.9). The weight loss was higher in mixed leaf litter (47 – 71%) than the single species leaf litter (44 – 62%) in all the experimental plots.

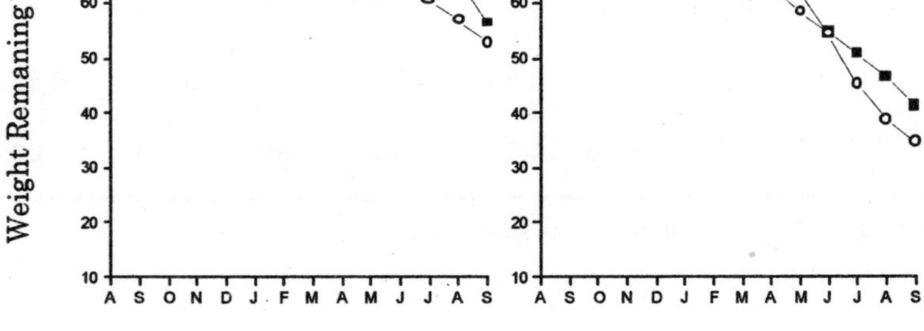

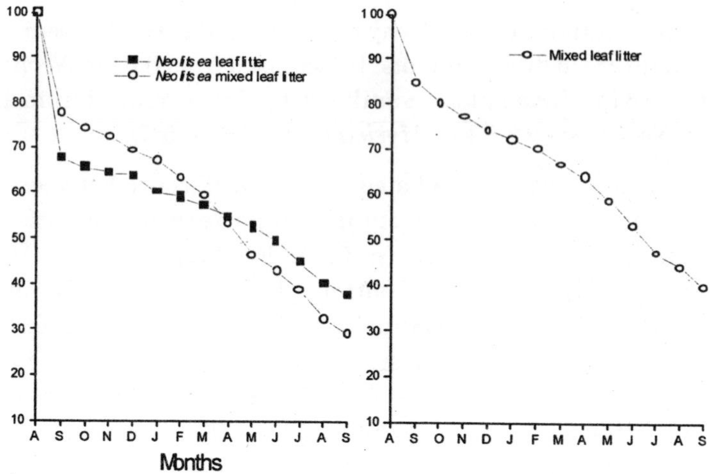

Figure 5.2 Decay pattern of leaf litter of dominant tree species and mixed leaf litter (including leaf litter of dominant species) in the experimental plots

Table 5.7
Annual decay constant (k) of leaf litter of dominant tree species and mixed leaf litter in different experimental plots

Parameters	*Myrica*		*Rhododendron*		*Neolitsea*		*Mixed*
	Leaf litter	*Mixed leaf litter**	*Leaf litter*	*Mixed leaf litter**	*Leaf litter*	*Mixed leaf litter**	*Litter decay*
k	0.53	0.59	0.82	0.98	0.89	1.13	0.85
t_{50}	1.32	1.18	0.85	0.72	0.78	0.61	0.82
t_{99}	9.52	8.53	6.13	5.15	5.60	4.4	5.9

*Includes leaf litter of dominant species in the respective plots

Table 5.8
Mean weight loss (%) of leaf litter of dominant tree species and mixed leaf litter (including leaf litter of dominant tree species) in different experimental plots (each value is a mean of 39 measurements taken between September 2004 and September 2005)

Experimental plots	*Leaf litter of dominant tree species*	*Mixed leaf litter (including leaf litter of dominant tree species)*
Myrica	3.35[b,c]	3.63
Rhododendron	4.53[a,b]	5.02[b,d]
Neolitsea	4.78[a,c]	5.46[b,c]
Mixed	–	4.64[c, d]
LSD	1.45	0.85
Significance level	0.05	0.05

Values with similar superscript in the rows are not significant at $p<0.05$

Table 5.9
Analysis of variance of weight loss between litter types in different plots

Experimental plots	*Degrees of freedom*	*F value*	*p*
Myrica litter types	1	17.45	0.05
Rhododendron litter types	1	24.53	0.05
Neolitsea litter types	1	1191.58	0.05

Table 5.10

Relationship between weight loss of leaf litter of dominant tree species and soil properties and decay rate and chemical composition

Variables	*Regression Equation*	*Degrees of freedom*	*Correlation co–efficient (r)*	*p*
Weight loss vs. soil properties				
SMC	Y= –2.58+0.14 X	155	0.30*	<0.05
ST	Y= –4.90 + 0.52 X	155	0.35*	<0.05
pH	Y= 21.59 – 4.06 X	155	– 0.27*	<0.05
Decay rate vs. chemical composition				
N	Y= 0.64 + 0.08 X	35	0.14	0.47
C/N ratio	Y= 0.81– 0.001 X	35	– 0.11	0.59
Lignin	Y= 1.15 – 0.01 X	35	– 0.48**	<0.01
Lignin/N	Y= 0.81 – 0.003 X	35	– 0.17	0.40

* Significant at p<0.05

** Significant at p<0.01

Table 5.11

Relationship between weight loss of mixed leaf litter (including leaf litter of dominant tree species) and soil properties, decay rate, and chemical composition

Variables	*Regression Equation*	*Degrees of freedom*	*Correlation co–efficient (r)*	*p*
Weight loss vs. soil properties				
SMC	Y= –0.36+0.02 X	155	0.50*	<0.05
ST	Y= –0.48 + 0.06 X	155	0.48*	<0.05
pH	Y= 2.35 – 0.41 X	155	– 0.32*	<0.05
Decay rate vs. chemical composition				
N	Y= 0.53 + 0.26 X	35	0.36*	<0.05
C/N ratio	Y= 1.19 – 0.01 X	35	– 0.35*	<0.05
Lignin	Y= 1.12 – 0.01 X	35	– 0.31	0.06
Lignin/N	Y= 0.98 – 0.004X	35	– 0.23	0.18
Weight loss vs. species richness				
Species richness	Y= 3.88 + 0.15 X	155	0.05	0.51

* Significant at p<0.05

Discussion

Litter production in forest ecosystems depends on several ecological factors; e.g. climate, species composition, stands age and site quality (Haase1999, Sundarapandian and Swamy 1999, Norgrove and Hauser 2000, Yang *et al.* 2004a, 2005). The values of annual total litterfall obtained in the present study (9,535 – 12,827 kg $ha^{-1}yr^{-1}$) are within the range reported from Amazonian tropical forest (2,400 – 10,300 kg $ha^{-1}yr^{-1}$) (Cuevas and Medina 1986), tropical evergreen forest (9,700 – 14,200 kg $ha^{-1}yr^{-1}$) and moist deciduous forest (13,000 – 15,000 kg $ha^{-1}yr^{-1}$) of Indian Western Ghats (Swamy and Procter 1994) and tropical dry evergreen forest (13,300 – 13,500 kg $ha^{-1}yr^{-1}$) of India (Arul Pragasan and Parthasarathy 2005). The results of present study is also comparable to the value (11,902 kg $ha^{-1}yr^{-1}$) reported by Arunachalam (1996) from a 7-year-old regrowth of subtropical forest in Meghalaya.

Facelli and Pickett (1991) reported that species composition is important for litter production within the same climate range. Significantly ($p<0.05$) high litterfall in *Rhododendron* plots as compared to other experimental plots could be partly due to the inherent characteristics of the tree species, their density and diverse responses of species to different environmental factors (Issac and Nair 2006, Yang *et al.* 2005, George and Kumar 1998).

The proportion of leaf (71 – 81%) in the litterfall is similar to those reported by Lian and Zhang (1998) from subtropical evergreen forest of China (50 – 80%), by Arunachalam (1996) from subtropical forest regrowth in Meghalaya (78 – 88%) and by Haase (1999) from tropical rain forest in Malaysia (71%) and Venezuela (74%). The percentage contribution of branches and miscellaneous litter (15 – 29%) in the present study was higher compared to those reported by Arunachalam (1996) (9 – 16%), but close to those reported by Mehra *et al.*

(1985) from Central Himalayan forest (9 – 20%) and by Yang *et al.* (2005) from seven natural forest of subtropical China (10 – 26%).

The seasonal pattern of litterfall is related to seasonal changes in climatic variables, such as temperature and moisture, and intrinsic genetic character of species (Jamaludheen and Kumar 1999). The peak litterfall observed in March (spring) in the present study is similar to the observation of studies in evergreen broadleaved forest Khiewtam and Ramakrishnan (1993), Arunachalam (1996) and Yang *et al.* (2004a). Another peak of litterfall observed in August in *Myrica, Rhododendron* and *Neolitsea* plots is attributed to high rainfall during this month.

The litter accumulation value obtained (4,334 – 6,147 kg ha^{-1}) in the present study is close to those reported from tropical dry evergreen forest (4,100 – 4,900 kg ha^{-1}; Arul Pragasan and Parthasarathy 2005) and tropical forest (3,800 – 5,500 kg ha^{-1}; Sundarapandian and Swamy 1999) of Indian Western Ghats , semi deciduous forest of Brazil (5,500 kg ha^{-1}; Morellato 1992) and *Dalbergia sissoo* forest of different ages in Central Himalaya, India (4,800 – 6,600 kg ha^{-1}; Lodhiyal *et al.* 2002) but lower than those reported from lowland rainforest of Nigeria (8,300 – 9,400 kg ha^{-1}; Odiwe and Muoghalu 2003), tropical wet evergreen forest and semi-evergreen forest of Western Ghats, India (11,700 and 10,400 kg ha^{-1}; Parthasarathy 1992).

The greater litter accumulation in *Myrica* plots was due to slow decomposition rate (0.53) and turnover rate (2.04 yr^{-1}). On the contrary, lower litter accumulation in *Neolitsea* and mixed plots was due to faster decomposition and turnover rate. This finding is consistent with the studies of Vogt *et al.* (1986), where rapid decomposition of litter has been attributed as an important cause of lower litter accumulation on the forest floor of wet tropical forest. Arul Pargasan and

Parthasarathy (2005) also reported that the significant differences in total litter accumulation between two tropical dry evergreen forest sites on the Coromandel coast of south India, was related to differences in temperature, soil moisture and decomposition rates besides vegetation variables. The high accumulation of litter in *Rhododendron* plots could be attributed to vegetation characteristics. This is further supported by a significant positive correlation between tree density and littermass ($Y = -8.42 + 0.004 X$, $r = 0.61$, $p < 0.05$).

The decomposition rates (k values: 0.53 — 1.13) of leaf litter falls within the range reported from semi–evergreen tropical forests of Grande-Terre, Guadeloupe, French West Indies (k= 0.41 – 2.39; Loranger *et al.* 2002), Nokrek Biosphere Reserve in Meghalaya (k= 0.88 – 1.76; Ralte 2004) but higher than those reported from subtropical evergreen broad-leaved forest on Okinawa Island, Japan (k= 0.22 – 0.84; Xu and Hirata 2005). The findings of the present study revealed that weight loss of mixed leaf litter was faster than the single species leaf litter. This is attributed to the higher N concentration and lower lignin in mixed leaf litter than single species leaf litter. This provides support to the hypothesis that litter mixtures decompose faster than expected when the mixture contains litter types with a very different N concentration, where one of the species had a much higher litter N concentration than the other. This is also in agreement with the findings of Hector *et al.* (2000) that synergistic effects of litter mixing enhance decomposition. Conn and Dighton (2000) reported that mass loss was enhanced when oak litter was present in pure pine litter. Salamanca *et al.* (1998) found that the decomposition of two species mixtures of litter was greater than predicted from single species litter bags. In an experiment with high diversity mixtures, Bardgett and Shine (1999) found a general increase in decomposition rate with increasing litter diversity due to synergistic, non-additive effects of litter mixing. Blair *et al.* 1990, McTiernan *et al.*

1997, Wardle *et al.* 1997b and Chapmann *et al.* 1988 have found strong, non–additive effects on decomposition rates of mixed litters that were both positive and negative. These non–additive effects have been suggested to arise in part from translocation of nutrients or inhibitory compounds between species. Movement of nutrients from one species to another in mixtures of litter is thought to relax nutrient limitation in the decomposer community, increasing overall decomposition (Chapmann *et al.* 1988, Blair *et al.* 1990, Wardle *et al.* 1997b). The nutrients could aid the decomposition of other species in the mixture, and are supposedly translocated from one litter type to another by diffusion (through a water film) and/or active transport through the hyphae of fungi connecting two different litter types (McTiernan *et al.*1997).

Non-additive (both positive and negative) effects of litter mixing have largely been attributed to plant species traits, in particular N concentration (Swift *et al.* 1979). However, in the present study it was found that the decomposition rate of the individual litter was not significantly related to their N content or C/N ratio, but when mixed, synergistic interactions between species of different N content might have occurred. Wardle *et al.* (1997b) showed that when litter of plants with high N status was mixed, synergistic effects on decomposition rate were observed. Seastedt (1984) also suggested that litter of higher quality is likely to enhance the decomposition of other litters, while poor quality litter may have negative effects. It is also likely that the non-additive interactions may be related to other plant species traits, such as initial lignin and cellulose content (Wardle *et al.* 1997b)

In all the plots litter exhibited a conspicuous phase of rapid decomposition followed by stabilization. The faster initial phase which lasted for 1 – 2 months (August-October) coincides with the rainy season when conditions are favourable for decomposition. Faster initial rates in decomposition process may reflect the leaching of soluble compounds and the decay of easily degradable compounds and tissues (Swift *et al.* 1979, Loranger *et al.* 2002). After the initial faster phase, decomposition rate appeared to be rather constant.

Litter decomposition rates are frequently considered to be regulated by soil organisms, environmental conditions and chemical nature of the litter (Gallardo and Merino 1993). The physical environment, especially soil moisture, temperature and relative humidity are important in litter decay as these regulate the biological activity in soil. The weight loss pattern of leaf litter of dominant tree species and mixed leaf litter in different plots was positively related to soil moisture and temperature and negatively to soil pH (Table 5.10 and 5.11). Lower decomposition rates in the *Myrica* plots compared to other plots may be attributed to the lower moisture content of the forest floor due to its openness. Likewise lower litter decomposition rates were found in clear-cut areas (1– 97 ha) or in large gaps (>15 m diameter) than in small gaps and under close canopy (Zhang and Liang 1995, Prescott *et al.* 2000).

The annual decay constant (k) was negatively related to initial lignin, C/N and Lignin/N ratios and positively to initial N concentration. Thus, higher rate of decomposition of *Neolitsea* leaf litter was due to high N and low lignin concentration and C/N ratio, while lower rate of *Myrica* leaf litter was due to lower N concentration and higher lignin concentration and C/N ratio. The decomposition of leaf litter was regulated by soil temperature and moisture and lignin content (Table 5.10). The present finding is in agreement to those of Sariyildiz and Anderson (2003) that initial concentration of Klason lignin was the best predictor for mass losses from litter species and litter types. The higher decomposition of mixed leaf litter in *Neolitsea* plots is attributed to higher N concentration and lower lignin and C/

N ratio, while lower N and higher lignin and C/N ratio in *Myrica* plot mixed leaf litter could be the reason for lower decomposition. Thus, the decomposition of mixed leaf litter was influenced by soil moisture, temperature, N concentration and C/N ratio (Table 5.11).

The faster rate of decomposition of leaf litter and mixed leaf litter in *Rhododendron* plots in spite of lower N and higher C/N ratio than the *Myrica* plots could be attributed to higher soil moisture content, temperature, soil organic matter and microbial biomass in soil which might have favoured faster decomposition. This explains the importance of physical, chemical and biological properties of soil as well as a combination of quality and nature of litter in decomposition on the forest floor.

Though the present study showed positive effects of litter diversity on decomposition, the results did not show a significant positive relationship between the two. In an ecosystem context, the present study provide support to the conclusion of Wardle *et al.* (1997b) that the nature of effects of each species are likely to be related to its functional characteristics rather than diversity per se. The present findings are also in agreement with results of Knops *et al.* (2001) suggesting that plant species richness can influence decomposition by impacting the quality of litter and microclimate in which the litter decomposes.

However, there is no empirical or theoretical reason to believe that different ecological processes should all respond to diversity in a qualitatively similar way (Madritch and Cardinale 2007).

6

Fine Root Dynamics

Introduction

Fine roots are an important source and sink for nutrients in terrestrial ecosystems. Though they comprise only about 5% of the total biomass in a forest ecosystem, they contribute as much as 40% of the annual primary production and play a crucial role in nutrient dynamics within the ecosystem (Buyanovsky *et al.* 1987, Vogt *et al.* 1991, Lopez *et al.* 2001) by enriching the soil with organic matter and nutrients through their fast turnover rate, and prevent leaching losses of nutrients by efficient absorption. Fine roots are an accurate indicator of root function than large roots (Berish 1982). Across a range of ecosystems, net primary production can be greater in belowground than the above ground (Caldwell 1987). The nutrient concentrations in fine roots may be higher than those in foliage (Meier *et al.* 1985) and their life spans are considerably shorter (Vogt *et al.* 1983). Nutrient release from decomposing roots is a pathway of significant nutrient flux in terrestrial ecosystems (Joslin and Henderson 1987, Fahey *et al.* 1988). In forests, the amount of carbon and nutrients returned to the soil from fine root turnover may equal or exceed to that from leaf litter (Joslin and Henderson 1987, Raich and Nadelhoffer 1989).

Mc Claugherty *et al.* (1984) estimated that fine roots are the source of soil organic matter accounting for 25% in northern hardwoods to 36% in *Pinus resinosa* forest. Fine root production may also vary substantially from year to year. Persson (1983) observed much variation in fine root dynamics within as well as between species. Hendricks and Pregitzer (1993) stated that the differences in biomass turnover may be due to temporal variation in root production. There is a lot of variation in fine root biomass values among different forest types due to differences in methodology used, sampling time and definition of what constitutes a fine root (McClaugherty *et al.* 1984, Burke and Raynal 1994, Steele *et al.* 1997). In forest ecosystem where N is a limiting nutrient for plant growth, the supply of available N generated during N mineralization is of crucial importance. However, it is not clear whether or not the fine root turnover rate increases (Nadelhoffer *et al.* 1985, Roy and Singh 1995) or decreases (Keyes and Grier 1981) with higher nutrient availability. The emphasis of the present study was to examine the impact of change in tree species composition on dry matter production, accumulation and turnover of fine roots as well as their importance in enriching the soil through decomposition in a humid subtropical forest ecosystem. The data pertaining to the above aspects have been presented in this chapter.

Methods

Root sampling

In each permanent plot, three replicated soil samples were collected using a steel corer (10 cm diameter) from the surface soil layer (0–10 cm depth) on monthly basis during one annual cycle from September 2004 to September 2005. The samples were taken to the laboratory in polythene bags and stored in a deep freeze at –20^{0}C before root separation. Roots were retrieved from the soil cores by wet– sieving method outlined by Bohm (1979) and processing of all samples were completed within 21 days as suggested by Parrotta and Lodge (1991).

The separated roots were assigned to two diameter classes: <2 and 2–15 mm, using a vernier caliper. In each class, live and dead roots were distinguished based on pliability and the degree of cohesion between the cortex and periderm. Live roots were often smooth and light coloured as compared to the dead roots that were wrinkled and dark in colour (Persson 1983). Fine (<2mm) and coarse (>2–15mm) roots were washed twice to ensure removal of all adhering soil particles.

The clean root samples were dried to a constant weight at 80^{0}C for 48 hours and weighed. Annual root production was determined by summing up the positive increments in live root biomass in each diameter class and concurrent increment, if any, in the dead root mass in a given diameter class during successive samplings (Persson 1978).

Fine root decomposition

Roots in upper soil layer (0–10 cm) were also collected in bulk separately from all the permanent plots during June 2004.They were carefully washed under a gentle flow of tap water to remove adhering soil and accompanying organic debris and separated into live and dead portions according to Persson (1982). Due to difficulty in collecting sufficient amount of newly senesced fine roots, live roots measuring <2 mm in diameter were separated, air dried and used for decomposition studies by litter bag technique (Mc Claugherty *et al.* 1984).

Three grams air–dried root material was placed in each nylon bag (1mm mesh, size 15cm×15cm). Forty such bags were buried in surface soil layer during August 2004 in each plot. Subsamples of air dried materials were taken in triplicate from each plot for dry weight determination. Three bags were retrieved from each plot monthly. The sample from each bag was cleaned to remove the adhering plant parts and soil particles, oven dried at 80°C for 48 hr and weighed. The dried samples were powdered in a CYCLOTEC (Tecator) for the determination of chemical composition.

Nutrient analysis

The ash content was determined by igniting the sample at 550°C for 6 hours in a muffle furnace. Carbon content was calculated as 50% of the ash free weight. Nitrogen and phosphorus contents were determined according to Allen *et al.* (1974) and lignin was determined following the method outlined by Peach and Tracey (1956).

Root turnover

Litter turnover rate (k) was calculated using mathematical model of Reiners and Reiners (1970)

$$k = P / X_m$$

Where, P= annual production (kg ha^{-1} yr^{-1}) and X_m= Mean annual drymass (kg ha^{-1})

Turnover time (T) was calculated as a reciprocal of turnover rate

T= 1/k, where, T= time in year.

Annual decomposition rate constant (k) was calculated using data on the percent mass remaining using the negative exponential decay model (Olson 1963)

$$k = (\ln (x/x_o))/t$$

Where, x_o= initial dry weight; x= weight remaining at the end of the investigation and t is the time in years. The time required for 50% (t_{50}) and 99% (t_{99}) decay and mineralization were calculated as $t_{50} = 0.693/k$ and $t_{99} = 5/k$.

Statistical analysis

The data was analysed using two-way ANOVA to test

the effect of months and tree species on production, drymass and weight loss of fine roots. Fisher LSD test was carried out to compare the mean values. Correlation analysis was carried according to Zar (1974).

Results

Fine root drymass

Mean annual drymass ranged from 3,964 – 4,676 $kgha^{-1}$. Among the experimental plots, fine root drymass was significantly ($p<0.001$) high in *Rhododendron* plots than the other three plots, but it was not different among the other three plots. The order of fine root drymass among the plots was *Rhododendron* > Mixed ≥ *Neolitsea* ≥ *Myrica* (Table 6.1).

Monthly variation in fine root drymass was similar in all the experimental plots (Figure 6.1). It started decreasing from July to November-December, when the lowest value was obtained; it then increased gradually from January to reach the peak in July.

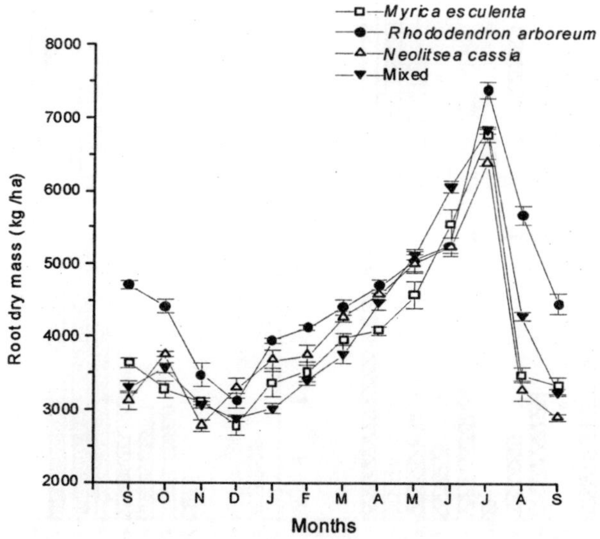

Figure 6.1 Monthly variations in fine root dry mass in different experimental plots

Fine Root production

Mean annual production of fine roots ranged between 4,297 – 4,431 kg ha^{-1}yr^{-1} with highest value in *Rhododendron* plots (4,431 kg ha^{-1}yr^{-1}) and lowest in Mixed plots (4,297 kg ha^{-1}yr^{-1}). It showed wide monthly fluctuations in all the plots, with peak values during rainy season (June-July). During autumn and winter seasons no positive increment was observed (Figure 6.2).

The turnover rate varied between 0.95 – 1.10 and it was in order: *Neolitsea* > *Myrica* > Mixed > *Rhododendron*. The turnover time varied from 0.91yr in *Neolitsea* to 1.05 yr in *Rhododendron*.

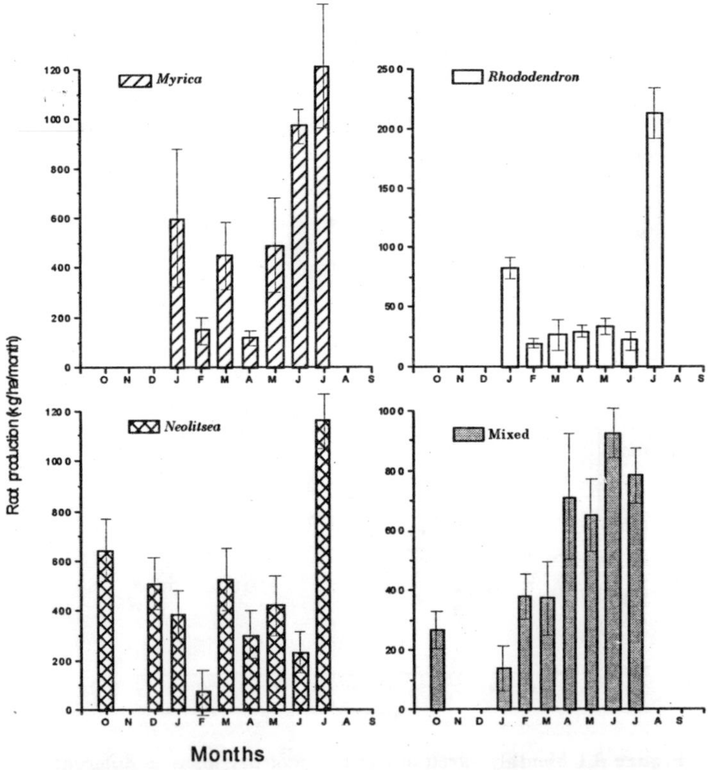

Figure 6.2 Monthly fine root productions in different experimental plots

Table 6.1
Mean annual dry mass (kg ha^{-1}), production (kg $ha^{-1}yr^{-1}$), turnover rate (k, yr^{-1}) and turnover time (t, yr) of fine roots in different experimental plots

Experimental plots	*Mean annual dry mass (kg ha^{-1})*	*Production (kg $ha^{-1}yr^{-1}$)*	*Turnover rate (k, yr^{-1})*	*Turnover time(t)*
Myrica	3,963.60[b,c]±115.25	4,319.90[b]	1.09	0.92
Rhododendron	4675.50±104.09	4431.30[a]	0.95	1.05
Neolitsea	4009.69[a,b]±101.86	4420.30[a]	1.10	0.91
Mixed	4084.05[a,c]±71.13	4297.20[b]	1.05	0.95
LSD	152.62	38		
Significance level	0.05	0.05		

Values with similar superscripts in the rows are not significant at $p<0.05$

Initial chemical composition of pre-decomposing fine root

Carbon content in fine root litter did not vary much between the plots. Nitrogen content however, varied from a minimum of 0.48% in *Myrica* plots to a maximum of 1.22% in *Neolitsea* plots. Phosphorus content was low in all the plots and varied from a maximum of 0.069% in Mixed plots to a minimum of 0.018% in *Myrica* plots. C/N ratio was minimum (37.87) in *Neolitsea* plots and maximum (88.88) in *Myrica* plots. Fine roots of Mixed plots (18.87%) had low lignin content whereas those of *Myrica* plots had high (25.78%) content (Table 6.2).

Table 6.2
Initial chemical composition of pre-decomposing root in different experimental plots (± SE, n=3)

Experimental plots	*C (%)*	*N (%)*	*P (%)*	*Lignin (%)*	*C/N*	*Lignin/ N*
Myrica	42.96± 0.15	0.48± 0.02	0.018± 0.002	25.78± 0.48	89.5± 3.24	53.34± 2.88
Rhododendron	46.53± 0.33	0.58± 0.07	0.037± 0.001	24.32± 1.17	80.22± 10.06	42.73± 4.81
Neolitsea	46.06± 0.05	1.22± 0.02	0.059± 0.001	20.77± 0.39	37.75± 0.52	17.07± 0.24
Mixed	43.17± 1.33	1.15± 0.13	0.069± 0.001	18.87± 1.13	37.54± 5.60	17.03± 2.82

Decomposition of fine roots

Fine roots showed three distinct phases of decomposition (Figure 6.3). The first phase lasting for about 60 days was characterized by a rapid rate of decomposition (10 –13% weight loss). This was followed by a period of slow weight loss lasting for another 200 days (5 – 7% weight loss). During the third phase i.e., between 270 and upto 400 days, decomposition was faster (10 – 15% weight loss) than during the second phase. The percentage of the original mass lost after 400 days of decomposition ranged from 30.33% in *Myrica* plots to 39% in Mixed plots.

There was a significant difference between the months in weight loss but difference between the experimental plots was not significant (Table 6.4). The decay constant varied from 0.33 to 0.45 and the plots may be ranked as Mixed > *Rhododendron* > *Neolitsea* > *Myrica*. The time required for 50% decay (t_{50}) increased from 1.54 in Mixed to 2.09 in *Myrica* plots. Similarly, t_{99} also increased from 11.11 in Mixed plots to 15.15 in *Myrica* plots (Table 6.3).

Table 6.3
Annual decay constant (k) of fine roots in different experimental plots

Parameters	*Myrica*	*Rhododendron*	*Neolitsea*	*Mixed*
Root decay				
k	0.33	0.39	0.38	0.45
t_{50}	2.09	1.78	1.82	1.54
t_{99}	15.15	12.82	13.16	11.11

Table 6.4
Analysis of variance showing effect of months and experimental plots on weight loss

Source of Variance	*Degrees of freedo*	*F value*	*p*
Months	12	35.26*	0.05
Experimental plots	3	1.99	0.11

* significant at $p<0.05$

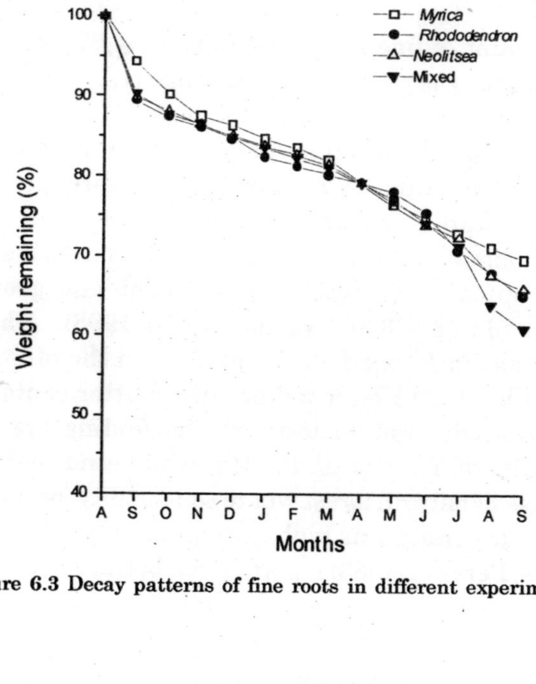

Figure 6.3 Decay patterns of fine roots in different experimental plots

Table 6.5
Relationship between weight loss of root and soil properties and decay rate and chemical composition

Variables	*Regression Equation*	*Degrees of freedom*	*Correlation co-efficient (r)*	*p*
Weight loss vs. soil properties				
SMC	Y= –0.50 + 0.03X	155	0.48*	<0.05
ST	Y= –0.89 + 0.11X	155	0.53*	<0.05
pH	Y= 4.31 – 0.77X	155	– 0.37*	<0.05
Decay rate vs. chemical composition				
N	Y= 0.32 + 0.08X	35	0.55*	<0.05
C/N ratio	Y= 0.38 + 0.001X	35	0.10	0.55
Lignin	Y= 0.62 – 0.01X	35	– 0.61*	<0.05
Lignin/N	Y= 0.45 – 0.001X	35	– 0.65*	<0.05

* Significant at $p<0.05$

Discussion

The amount of fine root mass (3,964 – 4,676 kg ha^{-1}) in the present study is well within the range (1,100 – 10,600 kg ha^{-1}) reported from other subtropical forests (Vogt *et al.* 1996, Yang *et al.* 2002, 2004b). It is comparable to those reported from *Picea abies* stand of Swedish natural forest (4,920 kg ha^{-1}; Majdi and Persson 1995), broad leaved humid subtropical forest (4,254 – 5,886 kg ha^{-1}; Arunachalam 1996) and subtropical pine forest of different age groups of Meghalaya (3,212 – 3,384 kg ha^{-1}; John 1998). The high fine root mass in *Rhododendron* plots than the other three plots could be due to high soil organic matter content and greater species diversity in the plot. This finding are similar to the results of Yang *et al.* (2004b) who found higher fine root biomass in natural forest where soil fertility, productivity and species diversity was high as compared to monoculture plantations. Persson (1983) reported that better soil conditions promote faster development of fine roots. Further the positive correlation between fine root mass and tree density (Y= –54.55 + 0.16X; r= 0.85; $p<0.001$) corroborate the findings of Arunachalam (1996) and Visalakshi (1994) that plant density and basal area also influence the fine root mass.

The annual fine root production obtained in the present study (4,297 – 4,431 kg $ha^{-1}yr^{-1}$) is within the range reported from different forest types. It is close to those reported from two evergreen forest (pine and oak) of Central Himalayas (3,706 –5,156 kg $ha^{-1}yr^{-1}$, Usman *et al.* 1999), broad leaved humid subtropical forests of Meghalaya, (4,240 – 5,690 kg $ha^{-1}yr^{-1}$, Upadhaya *et al.* 2005), *Castanopsis kawakamii* forest of subtropical China (4,410 kg $ha^{-1}yr^{-1}$, Yang *et al.* 2004b), dry tropical forest of Central India (1,780 – 5,910 kg $ha^{-1}yr^{-1}$, Roy and Singh 1994), evergreen (4,760 kg $ha^{-1}yr^{-1}$) and deciduous (5,268 kg $ha^{-1}yr^{-}$) tropical forests of Western Ghats (Sundarapandian *et al.* 1999) and temperate forest (1,600 – 5,910 kg $ha^{-1}yr^{-1}$, Nadelhoffer *et al.* 1985), montane Mediterranean forest (*Quercus ilex*) (4,000 kg $ha^{-1}yr^{-1}$, Canadell and Roda 1991), and *Eucalyptus globules* plantation (3,000–4,000 kg $ha^{-1}yr^{-1}$, Fabiao *et al.*1995).

Seasonal variation in fine root mass observed in tropical forests has been related to soil moisture and soil temperature conditions (Srivastava *et al.* 1986, Sundrapandian *et al.* 1999). High fine root biomass during rainy season indicated favourable period of root growth when availability of water and nutrients for growth in soil was high and temperature was optimum. Apart from soil conditions, phenology also coincided with the active phase of shoot growth. The low fine root mass during spring, which marks the initiation of new shoot growth after the dormant phase during winter was due to their slow growth in the preceding winter and the translocation of food reserves from the root system to shoot (Singh and Coleman 1997). A similar seasonal trend in root mass was also reported from subtropical humid forest of northeast India (Khiewtam and Ramakrishnan 1993, John *et al.* 2001, Upadhaya *et al.* 2005), dry tropical forest (Srivastava *et al.* 1986) and from deciduous and evergreen forests of south India (Parthasarathy 1987, Vishalakshi 1994, Sundarapandian and Swamy 1996).

According to Gill and Jackson (2000), fine root turnover rates of world forests were in the range of 0.02 to 2.64 yr^{-1}, with an average of 0.56 yr^{-1}. The present estimates (0.95 – 1.10 yr^{-1}) is within the range. However, it is slower than the growing stands of different ages of subtropical humid broad–leaved (0.64 – 0.73 yr^{-1}, Arunachalam 1996) and pine forests in Meghalaya (0.68 – 0.79 yr^{-1}, John 1998).

The values of annual decay constant (0.33 – 0.45) is within the range (0.02 – 3) as reported from different forest types across the world (Mc Claugherty *et al.* 1982, Anderson and Swift 1983, Bloomfield *et al.* 1993). Fahey and Hughes (1994) opined that low decomposition rate of fine roots could be its removal from the complex mycorrhizosphere environment that alter the normal decay process carried out by rhizosphere organisms or perhaps by mycorrhizal fungi.

The weight loss pattern showed a seasonal trend characterized by a faster rate of decay during the warm humid period and a slow decay rate during the dry cold period. Seasonal change in root decomposition rate in the tropical forest ecosystems is related to the soil moisture condition, ambient temperature and microbial activity (Swift *et al.* 1979). This is evident from positive relationship between weight loss and soil moisture and soil temperature. Low pH which retards microbial activity responsible for litter decay could be the probable reason for negative relationship between soil pH and weight loss. The rapid weight loss (10 – 13 %) at the initial phase (upto 60 days) coincided with the rainy season which affects large number of processes such as utilization of readily available energy sources by microbes, leaching of water soluble organic compounds, inorganic salts and non structural carbohydrates from the decomposing root litter (Bloomfield *et al.* 1993, Arunachalam *et al.* 1996, Cornu *et al.* 1997, John *et al.* 2002). With time the decay rate decrease as the proportion of more resistant materials like lignin and cellulose increases in the decomposing litter (Fogel and Cromack 1977).

The annual decay constant (k) was negatively related to initial lignin, C/N and Lignin/N ratios and positively to initial N concentration. Thus higher rate in Mixed and *Neolitsea* plots was due to high N and low lignin concentration and C/N ratio, while lower rate in *Myrica* plots was due to lower N concentration and higher lignin concentration and C/N ratio.

7

Nitrogen and Phosphorous Input, Accumulation and Release Through Litter and Fine Roots

Introduction

In forest ecosystem, litterfall is the largest source of organic material and nutrients for the humus layer. The quality and quantity of litterfall influences nature of the microbial community, including its size, composition, function and physiological properties. The composition of the microbial community may, in turn, influence the course of decomposition. All plant litter contains essential nutrients such as N, P, S, K, Ca, Mg, Mn and Fe, but their concentrations vary with the species. Thus, species are the dominant factor in determining the nutrient levels in litter; however, climate and composition of the mineral soil, parent material and the humus are also important.

At the ecosystem level, nutrient cycling is strongly affected by litter decomposition (Vitousek *et al.* 1994, Aerts and de Caluwe 1997). On the forest floor, litter acts as an input–

output system for nutrients, serving as a temporary sink for nutrients such as nitrogen (N), sulfur (S), and phosphorus (P), though the rate at which nutrients are released from litter is generally governed by the rate of decomposition. Various nutrients are released at different rates and may exhibit differential immobilization and release patterns. As the decomposition process progresses the chemical composition of litter changes. These changes are not, in all cases, linearly associated with mass loss. Neither are the changes in composition same for similar litter substrates decomposing under different environmental conditions. Thus, there is a complex and interacting set of factors that regulate mass loss, humus formation, nutrient dynamics and patterns of change in chemical composition of decomposing plant litter (Berg and Mc Claugherty 2003).

Changes in plant community composition may alter C and nutrient cycling through interspecific difference in rates of decomposition and nutrient release with possible feedbacks to soil processes (Hobbie 1992, 1996).

Nitrogen dynamics during litter decomposition is a complex process (Berg and Staaf 1981, Aber and Melillo 1982). The dynamics of other nutrients in decomposing litter are also complex, as they often occur in different forms and are subject to various transformations. Net immobilization of nutrients, often regulated by carbon: nutrient and nutrient: nutrient ratios may occur during litter decay (Upadhaya and Singh 1989). Because of this key role of litter decomposition, factors influencing litter quality and production have important implications for long–term productivity of forest ecosystems (Adàms and Angradi 1996).

Litter decomposition involves two simultaneous and fundamental sets of processes (Cou^teaux *et al.* 1995): 1) the mineralization and humification of lignin, cellulose, and other compounds by the action of a succession of microorganisms and 2) the leaching of soluble compounds into the soil profile. Mineralization of litter nutrients is often referred to a three-stage process: first, nutrients in soluble form are leached from the litter; second, nutrient immobilization occurs; and finally, net nutrient litter mineralization takes place, thereby making nutrients available for plant uptake again (Aerts and Chapin 2000).

To examine the influence of tree diversity on these attributes of the community data on N and P input, accumulation and release through litter and fine roots were collected and have been discussed in this chapter.

Methods

The methods of determining input, accumulation and nutrient release during litter and fine root decay have been described in detail in Chapter 5 and Chapter 6.

Analysis of plant materials

The ash content was determined by igniting the sample at 550°C for 6 hours in a muffle furnace. Carbon content was calculated as 50% of the ash free weight. Nitrogen and phosphorus contents were determined according to Allen *et al.* (1974) and lignin was determined following the method outlined by Peach and Tracey (1956).

Annual N and P mineralization constants (k_N and k_P) were calculated by substituting dry weight with N and P contents in the formula $-k = (\ln(x/x_0))/t$ (Olson 1963)

Where, x_0= initial dry weight; x= weight remaining at the end of the investigation and t is the time in years (Singh and Shekhar 1989). The time required for 50% (t_{50}) and 99% (t_{99}) decay and mineralization were calculated as $t_{50} = 0.693/k$ and $t_{99} = 5/k$.

Statistical analysis

The data was analysed using ANOVA to test the effect of

tree species on nutrient release from decaying litter and fine root. Fisher LSD test was carried out to compare the mean values. Correlation analysis was carried according to Zar (1974).

Results

Initial chemical composition of leaf litter of dominant tree species

Carbon content in the leaf litter varied significantly from a minimum of 43.66% in *Neolitsea* to a maximum of 47.50% in *Myrica*. The Nitrogen content also varied significantly ($p<0.01$) between the species with a minimum value 0.90% in *Rhododendron* to a maximum of 1.57% in *Neolitsea*. Though phosphorus content was low in all the leaf litter, it was high (0.065%) in *Neolitsea* and low (0.04%) in *Rhododendron*. C/N ratio varied widely from a minimum of 27.80 in *Neolitsea* to a maximum of 51.66 in *Rhododendron*. The lignin content was also low in *Neolitsea* (22.14) and high in *Rhododendron* (35.36%) leaf litter (Table 7.1).

Initial chemical composition of mixed leaf litter (excluding the dominant tree species)

Carbon content in mixed leaf litter varied from 43.7% to 46.7% with high value in *Myrica* plot and low in the other three plots. Nitrogen content was low in *Rhododendron* plots (0.71%) and high in Mixed plots (1.63%) whereas, the phosphorus content varied from a low in *Myrica* and *Rhododendron* plots (0.03%) to a high content in Mixed (0.07%) and *Neolitsea* plots (0.05%). The C/N ratio varied widely from a minimum of 28.12 in mixed plots to a maximum of 64.32 in *Rhododendron* plots. Lignin content in mixed leaf litter varied between the plots with high value in *Rhododendron* (35.37%) followed by *Myrica* plots (31.38%), *Neolitsea* (22.72%) and Mixed plots (23.37%) (Table 7.1).

Nitrogen content in branches and miscellaneous litter fractions was low as compared to those of foliar litter and

Table 7.1
Chemical composition of litter in different experimental plots (±SE, n=3)

Experimental plots	*Litter types*	*C(%)*	*N(%)*	*P(%)*	*Lignin(%)*	*C/N*	*Lignin/N*
Myrica plot	*Myrica* leaf litter	47.50±0.29	1.27±0.10	0.043±0.001	33.21±0.27	37.40	26.15
	Mixed leaf litter	46.67±0.88	0.98±0.03	0.03±0.001	31.38±1.22	47.62	32.02
	Branches +misc.		0.47±0.02	0.015±0.002			
Rhododendron plot	*Rhododendron* leaf litter	46.16±0.17	0.90±0.05	0.04±0.001	35.36±1.16	51.29	39.29
	Mixed leaf litter	45.67±0.33	0.71±0.03	0.03±0.001	35.37±0.43	64.32	49.82
	Branches +misc.		0.53±0.02	0.016±0.003			
Neolitsea plot	*Neolitsea* leaf litter	43.66±0.88	1.57±0.02	0.065±0.001	22.14±0.37	27.81	14.10
	Mixed leaf litter	43.67±0.85	1.10±0.08	0.05±0.003	22.72±0.22	39.70	20.65
	Branches +misc.		0.59±0.01	0.025±0.002			
Mixed plot	Mixed leaf litter	45.84±0.08	1.63±0.04	0.07±0.003	23.37±0.41	28.12	14.34
	Branches +misc.		0.53±0.02	0.03±0.002			

varied from a minimum of 0.47% in *Myrica* plots to a maximum of 0.59% in *Neolitsea* plots. Similarly, phosphorus content (0.015% – 0.03%) in branches and miscellaneous litter fractions can be arranged in the order: Mixed $\geq$ *Neolitsea* > *Rhododendron* $\geq$ *Myrica* plots.

The chemical composition of pre-decomposing fine roots is given in Table7.2. Carbon content in fine root litter varied between 42.96% in *Myrica* to 46.53% in *Rhododendron* plot. The nitrogen concentration ranged from a minimum of 0.48% in *Myrica* to 1.22% in *Neolitsea* plots. However, phosphorus was low in all the plots and varied from a maximum of 0.07 % in Mixed plot to a minimum of 0.02% in *Myrica* plots. Similarly, C/N ratio was low (37.54) in Mixed plot and high (88.88) in *Myrica* plots. Fine roots of Mixed plots had low lignin content (18.87%) whereas those of *Myrica* plot had high content (25.78%) (Table 7.2).

Table 7.2

Chemical composition of pre-decomposing fine roots in different experimental plots (±SE, n= 5)

Experimental plots	*C (%)*	*N (%)*	*P (%)*	*Lignin (%)*	*C/N*	*Lignin/ N*
Myrica	42.96±	0.48±	0.018±	25.78±	89.5±	53.34±
	0.15	0.02	0.002	0.48	3.24	2.88
Rhododendron	46.53±	0.58±	0.037±	24.32±	80.22±	42.73±
	0.33	0.07	0.001	1.17	10.06	4.81
Neolitsea	46.06±	1.22±	0.059±	20.77±	37.75±	17.07±
	0.05	0.02	0.001	0.39	0.52	0.24
Mixed	43.17±	1.15±	0.069±	18.87±	37.54±	17.03±
	1.33	0.13	0.001	1.13	5.60	2.82

Table 7.3
Mean annual accumulation (kg ha^{-1}), input (kg $ha^{-1}yr^{-1}$), turnover rate (k, yr^{-1}) and turnover time (t, yr) of N and P through litter on the forest floor in different experimental plots

Experimental plots	*Litter types*	*Accumulation*		*Input*		*Turnover rate (k, yr^{-1})*	*Turnover time (t, yr)*
		N	P	N	P		
Myrica plot	Myrica leaf litter	46.99	1.59	87.65	2.96	1.86	0.54
	Mixed leaf litter	9.80	0.30	28	0.86	2.86	0.35
	Branches +Miscellaneous	4.98	0.16	9.27	0.30	1.86	0.54
	Total	61.77	2.05	124.92	4.12	2.04	0.49
Rhododendron plot	Rhododendron leaf litter	36.60	1.63	65.64	2.92	1.79	0.56
	Mixed leaf litter	5.82	0.25	25.06	1.06	4.30	0.23
	Branches +Miscellaneous	6.68	0.20	10.63	0.32	1.59	0.63
	Total	49.10	2.08	101.33	4.30	2.09	0.48
Neolitsea plot	Neolitsea leaf litter	25.85	1.07	98.89	4.09	3.82	0.26
	Mixed leaf litter	17.35	0.79	34.32	1.56	1.98	0.51
	Branches +Miscellaneous	7.79	0.33	10.47	0.59	1.50	0.67
	Total	40.46	1.77	103.37	4.67	2.51	0.40
Mixed plot	Mixed leaf litter	53.14	2.28	110.97	4.77	2.10	0.48
	Branches +Miscellaneous	5.69	0.32	14.45	0.82	2.54	0.40
	Total	58.83	2.60	125.42	5.59	2.20	0.45

Table 7.4
Mean annual accumulation (kg ha^{-1}) and input (kg ha^{-1}yr^{-1}) of N and P through fine roots and their turnover in different experimental plots

Parameters	*Myrica plot*	*Rhododendron plot*	*Neolitsea plot*	*Mixed plot*
Nutrient accumulation				
N	19.03	27.12	48.92	46.97
P	0.79	1.87	2.41	2.86
Nutrient input				
N	20.74	25.70	57.93	49.42
P	0.86	1.77	2.65	3.01
Turnover rate of N and P	1.08	0.95	1.10	1.05
Turnover time of N and P	0.92	1.06	0.91	0.95

Input and accumulation of N through litter and fine roots

N accumulation in litter ranged between 40.5 – 61.8 kg ha^{-1}. It decreased in the following order of: *Myrica* > Mixed > *Rhododendron* > *Neolitsea.* Accumulation in fine roots ranged from 19 – 48.9 kg ha^{-1}. It decreased in the following order: *Neolitsea* > Mixed > *Rhododendron* > *Myrica* plots.

The annual inputs of N through litter and fine roots showed a different trend. Input through litter varied from about 125 kg ha^{-1}yr^{-1} in Mixed and *Myrica* plots to low 103.4 kg ha^{-1}yr^{-1}in *Neolitsea* and 101.3 kg ha^{-1}yr^{-1} in *Rhododendron* plots. Input through fine roots ranged from 20.7 – 57.9 kg ha^{-1}yr^{-1}. N input decreased in the experimental plots in the following order: *Neolitsea*> Mixed> *Rhododendron*> *Myrica.*

Input and accumulation of P through litter and fine roots

The P accumulation pattern through litter showed a

different trend from that of N. It varied from 1.8 to 2.6 kg ha^{-1} with maximum in the Mixed plot and minimum in *Neolitsea*. The accumulation of P through fine roots showed wide variation from 0.8 to 2.9 kg ha^{-1}. The highest value was recorded in Mixed plot and decreasing order followed by *Neolitsea*, *Rhododendron* and *Myrica* plots.

Annual input of P through litter (4.1 – 5.6 kg ha^{-1}yr^{-1}) and fine roots (0.9 – 3 kg ha^{-1}yr^{-1}) followed a similar and it decreased in order: Mixed > *Neolitsea* > *Rhododendron* > *Myrica* plot.

Turnover rates of N and P through litter was slower (2 – 2.5 yr^{-1}) than those of fine roots (0.95 – 1.10 yr^{-1}). It was fast in *Neolitsea* plot both in litter and fine roots. Litter turnover was slow in *Myrica* plots and that of fine roots in *Rhododendron* plot. The turnover time through litter and fine roots ranged from 0.40 – 0.49 yr and 0.91 – 1.06 yr respectively.

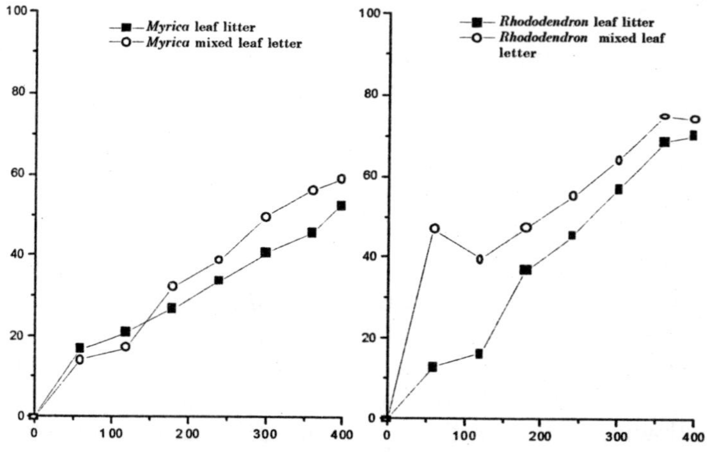

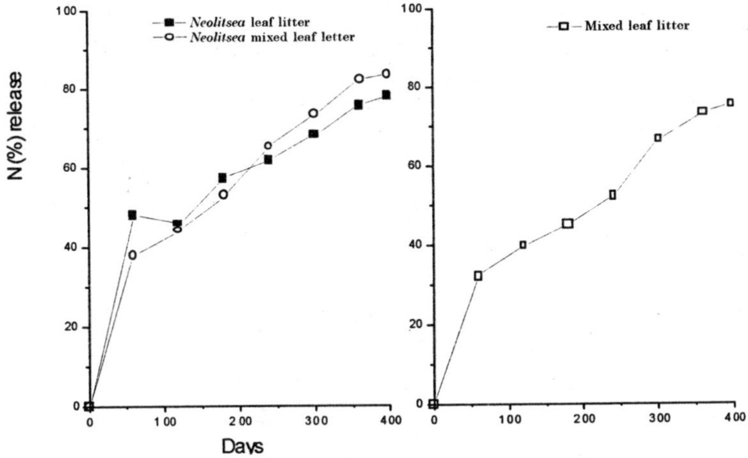

Figure 7.1 N release pattern from confined leaf litter in different experimental plots

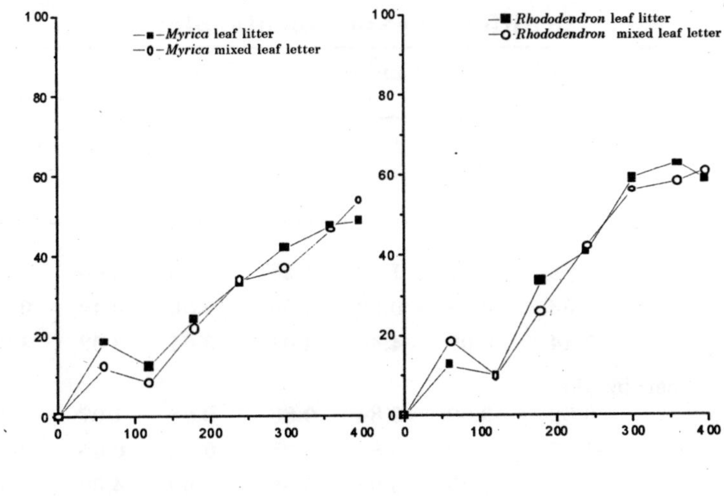

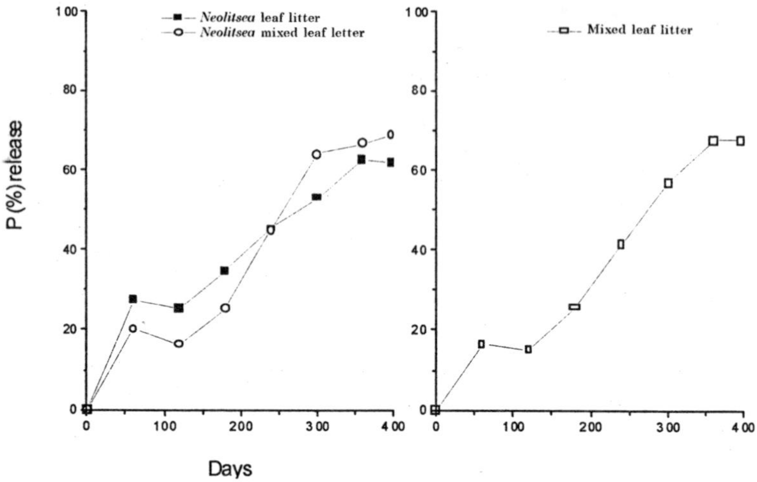

Figure 7.2 P release pattern from confined leaf litter in different experimental plots

Table 7.5
Annual mineralization constant (k_N and k_P) of leaf litter of dominant tree species and mixed leaf litter in different experimental plots

	Myrica plot		*Rhododendron plot*		*Neolitsea plot*		
Parameters	*Leaf litter*	*Mixed leaf litter**	*Leaf litter*	*Mixed leaf litter**	*Leaf litter*	*Mixed leaf litter**	*Mixed plot*
N mineralization							
k_N	0.68	0.82	1.12	1.25	1.39	1.66	1.29
t_{50}	1.03	0.85	0.62	0.56	0.50	0.42	0.54
t_{99}	7.44	6.09	4.46	4.01	3.61	3.02	3.88
P mineralization							
k_P	0.62	0.69	0.84	0.88	0.88	1.07	1.02
t_{50}	1.13	1.00	0.83	0.78	0.77	0.65	0.68
t_{99}	8.12	7.25	5.95	5.68	5.69	4.69	4.90

* Includes leaf litter of dominant species in the respective plots.

N and P release from confined leaf litter

Initially N release from decaying leaf litter was rapid, but it slowed down in all litters at about 120 days and continued till 400 days at differential rates. At the end of 400 days 53 – 78% of N had been released from the litter (Figure 7.1). The result showed a significant difference in N release rate between the months ($p<0.05$; $F= 25.40$) and plots ($p<0.05$; $F= 20.96$).

N mineralization constant of leaf litter varied from 0.68 to 1.39 with the highest value in *Neolitsea* leaf litter (k_N= 1.39), followed by *Rhododendron* plots (k_N= 1.12) and lowest in *Myrica* plots (k_N= 0.68). The N release pattern however, did not show significant variation ($p= 0.12$) in *Rhododendron* and *Neolitsea* leaf litter (Table 7.7).The time required for 50% mineralization (t_{50}) increased from 0.50 in *Neolitsea* to 1.03 in *Myrica* leaf litter. Similarly, t_{99} also increased from 3.61 in *Neolitsea* to 7.44 in *Myrica* leaf litter (Table 7.5).

However, P release was slower as compared to that of N but the trend was similar to that of N. After an initial rapid release phase, the period between 60 – 120 days was marked by no release of P in all litter (Figure 7.2). Two way ANOVA revealed significant variation ($p<0.01$) in P release rate between the months ($F= 53.74$) and plots ($F= 8.71$).

P mineralization constant varied from 0.61 to 0.88 with the highest value for *Neolitsea* leaf litter (k_p= 0.88), followed by *Rhododendron* (k_p= 0.84) and lowest for *Myrica* leaf litter (k_p= 0.61) (Figure 7.2) with 49%, 59% and 62% release respectively. The time required for 50% mineralization (t_{50}) increased from 0.77 in *Neolitsea* to 1.13 in *Myrica* leaf litter. Similarly, t_{99} also increased from 5.69 in *Neolitsea* to 8.12 in *Myrica* leaf litter (Table 7.5).

N and P release from confined mixed leaf litter

In this case, N and P mineralization continued until 400

days. However, the rate slowed down after initial rapid release phase (60 days). About 84% of initial N content was release in *Neolitsea* and 59% was released in *Myrica* plots during 400 days (Figure 7.1). The mixed leaf litter in *Neolitsea*, *Rhododendron* and Mixed plots had similar N release pattern (Table 7.7)

Mineralization constants (k_N and k_P) of mixed leaf litter was higher than the leaf litter of the dominant tree species (Table 7.5). N mineralization constant varied from 0.82 to 1.66 and it decreased in the following order *Neolitsea* > Mixed > *Rhododendron* > *Myrica*. The time required for 50% mineralization (t_{50}) increased from 0.42 yr in *Neolitsea* to 0.85 yr in *Myrica* plots. Similarly, t_{99} also increased from 3.02 in *Neolitsea* to 6.09 in *Myrica* plots (Table 7.5).

After 400 days 54 – 69% of the initial P content was released in all the plots (Figure 7.2), which showed a significant difference between them ($p<0.05$; $F= 11.25$). The rate of P release from mixed leaf litter was in the order *Neolitsea* ≥ Mixed ≥ *Rhododendron*> *Myrica* (Table 7.7). P mineralization constant of mixed leaf litter varied from 0.69 to 1.07 and the time required for 50% and 99% mineralization increased from *Neolitsea* to *Myrica* plot (Table 7.5).

Table 7.6

Annual mineralization constant (k_N and k_P) of fine roots in different experimental plots

Parameters	*Myrica plot*	*Rhododendron plot*	*Neolitsea plot*	*Mixed plot*
N mineralization				
k_N	0.60	0.78	0.85	0.68
t_{50}	1.16	0.89	0.82	1.02
t_{99}	8.35	6.41	5.88	7.37
P mineralization				
k_P	0.61	0.61	0.57	0.74
t_{50}	1.14	1.14	1.22	0.94
t_{99}	8.24	8.24	8.77	6.76

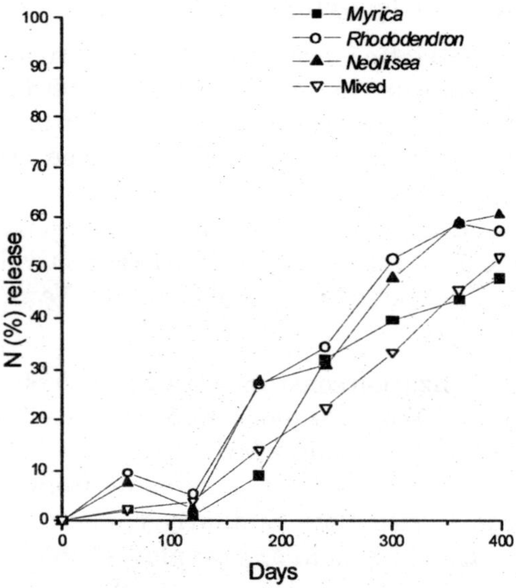

Figure 7.3 N release patterns from decaying fine roots in different experimental plots

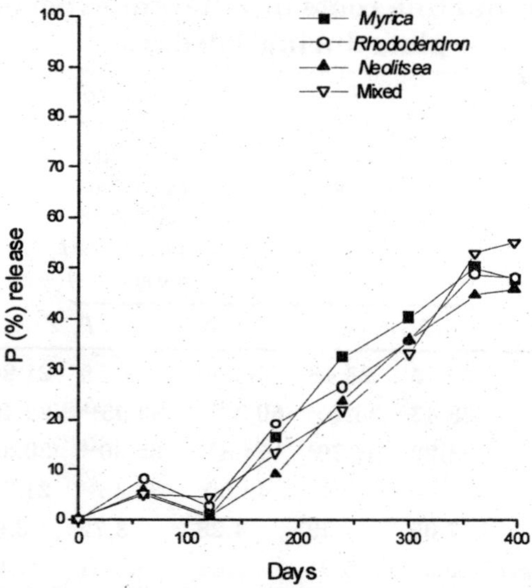

Figure 7.4 P release pattern from decaying fine roots in different experimental plots

N and P release from decaying fine roots

N and P mineralization from decaying fine root litter continued at different rates in different plots till 400 days. At the end of 400 days 48 – 61% of N was released from roots during decay. The rate was fast in *Neolitsea* and slow in *Myrica* plots (Figure 7.3). Two way ANOVA revealed significant variation ($p<0.01$) in N release pattern across the months and plots ($F= 114.93$ and $F= 10.51$ respectively). N release pattern of fine root litter was in the order *Neolitsea* > *Rhododendron* > *Myrica* ≥ Mixed (Table 7.7).

Nitrogen mineralization constant varied from 0.60 – 0.85 with higher value in *Neolitsea* plot which decreased in the following order of *Rhododendron* > Mixed > *Myrica*. The time required for 50% mineralization (t_{50}) increased from 0.82 in *Neolitsea* to 1.16 in *Myrica* plots. Similarly, t_{99} also increased from 5.88 in *Neolitsea* to 8.35 in *Myrica* plots (Table 7.6).

Table 7.7

N and P released (%) of initial content from decaying leaf litter and fine roots in different experimental plots during 400 days

Experimental plots	*Leaf litter of dominant tree species*		*Mixed leaf litter (including leaf litter of dominant tree species)*		*Fine root*	
	N	*P*	*N*	*P*	*N*	*P*
Myrica	29.73	28.48	33.50	26.75	21.90[a]	24.14
Rhododendron	38.43	34.70[a]	50.32[a,b]	33.95[a,b]	29.46[b]	23.68[a]
Neolitsea	54.22	38.79[a]	54.81[b]	38.30[a,c]	30.55[b]	20.72
Mixed	–	–	48.00[a]	36.38[b,c]	21.74[a]	23.24[a]
LSD	7.05	4.09	4.28	3.72	3.62	2.65
Significance level	<0.01	<0.01	<0.01	<0.01	<0.01	<0.01

[a,b,c] Values with similar superscript in the rows are not significant at $p<0.01$

Table 7.8
Relationship between weight remaining and nutrient mineralization and N and P concentration in decomposing litter (leaf litter of dominant tree species, mixed leaf litter and root) across the experimental plots

Variable	*Regression Equation*	*Degrees of freedom*	*Correlation coefficient (r)*	*Significance level (P)*
Leaf litter				
Weight remaining vs N mineralization	Y = 7.45 – 2.76X	26	– 0.97	<0.001
Weight remaining vs P mineralization	Y = 7.37 – 3.67X	26	– 0.73	<0.001
Mixed leaf litter				
Weight remaining vs N mineralization	Y = 7.54 – 2.89X	35	– 0.95	<0.001
Weight remaining vs P mineralization	Y = 4.68 – 0.86X	35	– 0.18	0.28
Fine root				
Weight remaining vs N mineralization	Y = 2.18 – 0.29X	35	– 0.30	0.07
Weight remaining vs P mineralization	Y = 2.59 – 1.01X	35	– 0.74	<0.001

The amount of P released during 400 days (46 – 55%) was similar to N during the study period (Figure 7.4). It showed a significant difference between the months ($p<0.05$; $F= 179.47$) and plots ($p<0.05$; $F= 2.02$). However, the difference between *Rhododendron* and Mixed plots was not significant (Table 7.7). The mineralization constant varied from a low of 0.57 in *Neolitsea* plots to a high of 0.74 in Mixed plots. The time required for 50% mineralization t_{50} increased from 0.94 in Mixed plots to 1.22 in *Neolitsea* plots (Table 7.6).

Discussion

N and P return through litter

The quantity of litter and its nutrient contents are major source through which nutrients cycle within forest ecosystem. The N input through litter (101.3 – 125.4 kg $ha^{-1}yr^{-1}$) in the present study is higher than those reported (27 – 88 kg $ha^{-1}yr^{-1}$) from different forest types (Issac and Nair 2006, Yang *et al.* 2005, Rapp *et al.* 1999). However, it is close to the values reported (101.8 – 153 kg $ha^{-1}yr^{-1}$) from tropical and subtropical forests (De Moraes *et al.* 1999, Arunachalam 1996). The P input through litter (4.1 – 5.6 kg $ha^{-1}yr^{-1}$) in the present study is close to those reported (2.4 – 8.7 kg $ha^{-1}yr^{-1}$) from different subtropical forest types (Yang *et al.* 2005, Arunachalam 1996). It is higher than those reported (1.5 – 4.2 kg $ha^{-1}yr^{-1}$) from different forest types (Issac and Nair 2006, Rapp *et al.* 1999, De Moraes *et al.* 1999).

N and P accumulation in litter (N: 40.5 – 61.8 kg ha^{-1}, P: 1.8 – 2.6 kg ha^{-1}) on the forest floor was higher than those reported (N: 10.5 – 22.1 kg ha^{-1}, P: 0.6 – 1.0 kg ha^{-1}) from broadleaved humid subtropical forest of Meghalaya (Arunachalam 1996).

Nutrient accumulation in litter is a function of its mass and concentration. Greater accumulation of N in litter in *Myrica* plot, in spite of low N concentration, is attributed to greater amount of litter on the forest floor which in turn was the result of slower rate of decomposition. In *Neolitsea* plot on the other hand, in spite of high N concentration in litter, lower amount in N littermass was primarily due to faster decay rate of weight loss. Greater input of N and P in Mixed plots could be attributed to high resource quality of the litter (De Moraes *et al.* 1999) whereas in *Myrica* plots it was related to production (Arunachalam 1996). Similarly, N and P accumulation was related to the nutrient concentration in case of Mixed, *Neolitsea* and *Rhododendron* in *Myrica* plots could be ascribed to the higher littermass. The observed differences in N and P input and accumulation in the present study is in agreement to the findings of Yang *et al.* (2005) who opined that the differences in the nutrient content of litter is due to the characteristics of the species. The amount of N returned to the forest floor through litter was greater than P in all the plots as also observed by Arunachalam *et al.* (1996b), Yang *et al.* (2005), Issac and Nair (2006). The difference in the amount of N and P return to the forest floor in different experimental plots reflects the influences of quantitative and qualitative variation in litter.

N and P return through fine roots

N input through fine roots (21 – 54 kg $ha^{-1}yr^{-1}$) of the present study is lower than those reported (44 – 184 kg $ha^{-1}yr^{-1}$) from different forest types (Mc Claugherty *et al.* 1982, Arunachalam 1996, John 1998). Input of P through fine roots (0.9 – 3 kg $ha^{-1}yr^{-1}$) of the present study is lower than reported (4 – 17 kg $ha^{-1}yr^{-1}$) from subtropical forest of Meghalaya (Arunachalam 1996, John 1998). Higher N and P concentration in the fine roots in *Neolitsea* and Mixed plots could be the reason for higher N and P input.

Accumulation of N through fine roots (19 – 49 kg ha^{-1}) in the present study is close to those reported (37 – 65 kg ha^{-1}) from different forest types (Mc Claugherty *et al.* 1982, Arunachalam 1996, John 1998). Similarly, the accumulation of P through fine roots (0.8 –3 kg ha^{-1}) in the present study is close reported (2.5 – 7 kg ha^{-1}) from subtropical forest of Meghalaya (Arunachalam 1996, John 1998).

Maximum accumulation and input of N in *Neolitsea* plots and P in Mixed plots can be ascribed to their high concentration. In all plots, the amount of N returned to the forest floor through fine roots was greater than P. This is consistent with the findings of Nambiar (1987), Khiewtam and Ramakrishnan (1993), Arunachalam (1996), John (1998).

N and P release through litter and fine roots

The decay of leaf and root litter showed three phases of N and P release in all the experimental plots. The initial phase of rapid nutrient release coincided with heavy period of summer rains which is helpful in leaching of the soluble nutrients. The second phase characterized by slower rate of nutrient release coincided with the dry winter season when microbial activities are at its minimum. Immobilization of nutrients in soil microbial biomass is the dominant process during this season. As decay advances, mineralization resulted in the decline of the nutrient in residual litter. Temporary immobilization of N and P noticed in decaying litter minimizes their losses from the ecosystem.

Myers *et al.* (1994) reported that low quality litter having high C/N ratio immobilizes N at a faster rate, while the high quality litter with low C/N ratio releases nutrient at a faster rate during decomposition. Thus, faster rate of N release from *Neolitsea* leaf litter could be due to its low C/N ratio (27.4) as compared to that of *Rhododendron* (C/N ratio 51.3) and *Myrica* (C/N ratio 37.4). Similarly, faster mineralization of N and P in decomposing leaf litter, mixed leaf litter and fine roots was due to better resource quality. In general, litter diversity affects the release of N, but different workers have obtained contradictory results. Blair *et al.* (1990) found that species diversity of litter have resulted in increased N mineralization while a decrease was observed by McTiernan *et al.* (1997). Wardle *et al.* (1997b) noted idiosyncratic patterns of N release with increasing litter diversity. The faster release of N and P from mixed leaf litter than the single species leaf litter is attributed to their high N and P concentration and lower lignin content.

Nutrient release is an ultimate reflection of weight loss of the litter. Thus, weight remaining was related to N and P mineralization of leaf and root litter that is observed from the negative correlation (Table 7.8). Therefore, factors which influence weight loss also affect mineralization of nutrients contained in the litter in situations where the release phase dominates the annual decomposition cycle. Positive relation (Table 7.8) between concentrations of pairs of nutrients during decomposition suggests that the behaviour of N and P were similar and might have influenced each other during decomposition (Xu and Hirata 2005).

8

Soil Microbial Biomass C, N and P and Nutrient Mineralization

Introduction

There is growing interest in understanding the linkages between forest dynamics and ecosystem processes because human induced changes in forest composition are likely to affect net primary productivity and patterns of nutrient cycling. Changes in plant community composition influence soil microbial communities in various direct and indirect ways. Tree species directly affect soil microbial communities through variations in litter quality (e.g. N, P, lignin, C:N), root activities (via root exudation of various compounds), complexity, and amount of organic input to soils. Plant characteristics (e.g. rooting depth and density, canopy cover) indirectly affect microbes via changes in the soil environment (e.g. soil moisture, temperature and soil pH) (Hooper *et al.* 2000). Soil microbes associated with different tree species often have variable amounts of microbial biomass (Bauhas *et al.* 1998, Templer *et al.* 2003), rates of nitrification (Finzi *et al.* 1998a, Menyailo *et al.* 2003, Brüggemann *et al.* 2005) and mineralization (Menyailo *et al.* 2003, Brüggemann *et al.* 2005).

Soil microbial biomass is also related to climate (Dyer *et al.* 1990), soil moisture (Taylor *et al.* 1999), soil texture (Bauhas *et al.* 1998, Hassink 1994, Wardle 1992), plant productivity (Zak *et al.* 1990, 1994) and organic matter quality (Taylor *et al.* 1989, Zak *et al.* 1990).

Soil microbes affect the availability of nutrients for uptake or loss through the process of mineralization and immobilization. A tight coupling between these processes could limit the pool size of soil N and P and accordingly reduce their loss from the soil. The balance between mineralization and immobilization is related to the quality of soil organic matter as well as the attributes of soil microbial community.

The effects of individual plant species are important determinants of ecosystem properties of organic matter decomposition and nutrient recycling (Grime 1997, Hooper and Vitousek 1997, Wardle *et al.* 1997b), since plant diversity has a positive effects on soil microbial processes (Stephan *et al.* 2000). Effect of tree species on soil microbial biomass C, N and P and N and P mineralization pattern was studied in humid subtropical forest of Meghalaya and results are discussed in this chapter.

Methods

Soil Microbial biomass

Microbial biomass in soils was determined in the upper soil layer (0–10 cm) at seasonal basis. Samples were collected in September (autumn season), December (winter season), March (spring season) and June (rainy season). At each sampling three samples were collected using soil corers (10 cm diameter) from permanent plot separately. The samples were sealed in polythene bags in the field and brought to laboratory. They were bulked to obtain composite samples for each plot, and sieved through 2mm mesh screen to remove stones, roots and plant debris. These field moist samples were used for the determination of microbial biomass carbon (MBC), nitrogen (MBN) and phosphorus (MBP).

Analysis

MBC was determined by chloroform fumigation extraction method (Vance *et al.* 1987b). Six sub-samples of 10 g ± 0.01 g each were drawn from each composite sample, three of them were fumigated by saturating with 10 ml (alcohol-free) chloroform liquid and kept for 24 hours and the remaining three were not fumigated. After fumigation, chloroform was removed from the samples by evaporation. Microbial biomass was extracted from both fumigated and non-fumigated samples with 50 ml of 0.5 M K_2SO_4 by shaking for 30 minutes. The extracts were filtered through Whatman filter paper No. 42 and the filtrates were used for the determination of microbial biomass carbon and nitrogen.

The organic C in the extracts of fumigated and non-fumigated soil samples was determined by digesting 4 ml filtered extract with 0.0667 M $K_2Cr_2O_7$ (1 ml) and 5 ml of H_2SO_4 (98% acid) for 30 minutes. The digested sample was titrated with acidified ferrous ammonium sulphate solution using 0.3 ml (3 – 4 drops) of indicator (o-phenanthroline monohydrate and ferrous sulphate hexahydrate). The MBC was calculated as

$$MBC = 2.64\ Ec$$

Where, Ec is the difference between the amount of organic C in the K_2SO_4 extract of fumigated and non-fumigated soils, both expressed as $\mu g\ g^{-1}$ dry soil, and 2.64 is the relationship between biomass C as measured by fumigation incubation method and amount of C extracted by 0.5 M K_2SO_4 after chloroform treatment.

MBN was determined by fumigation extraction method (Brookes *et al.* 1985) slightly modified by Okalebo *et al.*

(1993). For the estimation of N, 10 ml of the filtrate was digested at 350°C with 4.4 ml of digestion mixture (0.42 g selenium powder + 14 g lithium sulphate + 30 ml of 30% H_2O_2 + 420 ml conc. H_2SO_4) in a micro-Kjeldahl digestion tube till it becomes whitish or colourless. The mixture was extracted with distilled water in a 50 ml volumetric flask. The solution was filtered through Whatman No. 1 filter paper to get a clear solution for the estimation of MBN. Ten ml of clear extract was used to determine ammonium-N released as a result of reaction with 40% NaOH solution in the micro-Kjeldahl digestion chamber. The ammonium-N released was collected in 5 ml 1% boric acid solution till permanent green colour develops. Then, a few drops (2 – 4 drops) of bromocresol green indicator solution was added into the solution mixture and titrated with N/140 HCl till it turns into pink colour.

$$\text{MBN } (\mu g\ g^{-1} \text{ dry soil}) = N_f - N_o$$

Where, N_f = biomass N of fumigated sample; N_o = biomass N of non-fumigated sample

MBP was determined by chloroform fumigation extraction method (Brookes *et al.* 1982). Microbial biomass was extracted from both fumigated and non-fumigated samples with 50 ml of 0.5 M $NaHCO_3$ by shaking for 30 minutes. The extracts were filtered through Whatman filter paper No. 42 and the filtrates were analyzed for inorganic P using ammonium-molybdenum blue method (Allen *et al.* 1974).

The microbial biomass P was calculated as

$$\text{MBP} = b - a / 0.40$$

where, a = the amount of inorganic P ($\mu g\ g^{-1}$) extracted from unfumigated soil

b = the amount of inorganic P ($\mu g\ g^{-1}$) extracted from fumigated soil

0.40 = the fraction of biomass P mineralized and extracted in 0.5 M $NaHCO_3$

Net Nitrogen and Phosphorus mineralization

Net Nitrogen and Phosphorus mineralization were studied *in situ* by buried bags technique (Eno 1960) on monthly basis for one annual cycle during September 2004 to September 2005. At each sampling, paired soil cores were collected from the upper soil layer (0–10 cm) using a steel corer (10 cm diameter) randomly from three points in each permanent plot. One of the cores from each pair was sealed in sterilized polyethylene bags after removing roots and larger organic debris, and reinserted in soil at 0–10 cm depth. The other pair was brought to the laboratory and sieved through a 2 mm mesh screen. Initial moisture content (SMC), NH_4^+–N, NO_3^-–N and PO_4^{3-}–P concentrations were determined within 24 hours of sample collection following the method outlined by Allen *et al.* (1974). After one month, the buried bags were retrieved from each plot and soil samples were analysed for final NH_4^+–N, NO_3^-–N and PO_4^{3-}–P concentrations. Nitrification rates were calculated based on the changes in nitrate N concentrations by subtracting the initial concentration from their respective final concentration. Net nitrogen mineralization was calculated as the sum of changes in the extractable ammonium–N and nitrate–N over one month period. The increase in the concentration of phosphate–P during the field exposure is referred to as net phosphorus mineralization.

Statistical analysis

The data was analysed using two-way ANOVA to test the effect of seasons /months and tree species on soil microbial biomass, available nutrients and mineralization ratesl. Fisher LSD test was carried out to compare the mean values. Correlation analysis was carried according to Zar (1974).

Results

Microbial biomass carbon (MBC)

The MBC concentration ranged from 446 – 922 μg g^{-1} in

Rhododendron, 347 – 709 μg g^{-1} in *Neolitsea*, 258 – 463 μg g^{-1} in Mixed and 315 – 541 μg g^{-1} in *Myrica* plots (Table 8.1). The mean MBC was significantly ($p<0.001$) high in *Rhododendron* (700 μg g^{-1}) as compared to other three plots. However, difference between Mixed (390 μg g^{-1}) and *Myrica* plots (387 μg g^{-1}) was not significant (Table 8.5). The MBC showed a marked seasonal pattern in all the experimental plots, with peak during winter and trough during rainy season (Table 8.1).

The percentage contribution of MBC to SOC ranged between 1.37 – 2.26 %. Among the experimental plots, maximum contribution was observed in *Rhododendron* (2.26%) and minimum in the Mixed plots (1.37%) (Table 8.5). However, the contribution of MBC to SOC was similar in *Myrica* and Mixed plots.

Table 8.1
Seasonal variation in soil microbial biomass carbon (μg g^{-1}) in different experimental plots (±SE)

Experimental plots	*Autumn*	*Winter*	*Spring*	*Rainy*	*Autumn*
Myrica	336.78± 22.98	541.38± 45.86	390.20± 27.00	314.93± 33.24	349.87± 30.74
Rhododendron	487.11± 24.29	922.17± 149.54	882.10± 39.40	446.48± 23.56	766.88± 76.32
Neolitsea	471.11± 26.19	708.80± 43.29	573.46± 38.22	346.96± 45.87	507.85± 38.18
Mixed	404.90± 29.49	462.76± 53.78	445.05± 38.35	257.92± 7.58	380.30± 36.82

Microbial biomass nitrogen (MBN)

The MBN concentration ranged between 21 – 89 μg g^{-1}, with highest value in Mixed plots followed in decreasing order of *Neolitsea*, *Rhododendron* and *Myrica* plots (Table 8.5), however, there was no significant difference ($p<0.001$)

between Mixed and *Neolitsea* plots, and between *Neolitsea* and *Rhododendron* plots. The seasonal trend of MBN concentration was similar to that of MBC, with high values during winter and low during rainy season (Table 8.2). The percentage contribution of MBN to TKN ranged between 0.44% and 0.47% and did not vary significantly (p= 0.77) among the plots (Table 8.5).

Table 8.2
Seasonal variation in soil microbial biomass nitrogen ($\mu g\ g^{-1}$) in different experimental plots (±SE)

Experimental plots	*Autumn*	*Winter*	*Spring*	*Rainy*	*Autumn*
Myrica	23.12± 3.06	37.31± 2.47	28.79± 1.46	21.49± 2.26	21.90± 3.72
Rhododendron	22.71± 2.93	55.96± 6.44	41.37± 5.06	27.58± 4.93	26.77± 3.72
Neolitsea	22.71± 2.66	62.86± 7.04	47.85± 1.62	24.34± 2.43	26.77± 2.81
Mixed	27.58± 3.25	89.21± 0.81	42.18± 2.15	21.09± 2.93	29.20± 4.87

Microbial biomass Phosphorus (MBP)

The MBP concentration varied between 3.45 – 23.43 $\mu g\ g^{-1}$. Based on the concentration the experimental plots can be arranged in the following order: Mixed $\geq$ *Neolitsea* > *Rhododendron* > *Myrica* (Table 8.5). Its seasonal pattern was similar to MBC and MBN in all the experimental plots, with higher values during winter and lower during rainy (Table 8.3).

Table 8.3
Seasonal variation in soil microbial biomass phosphorus (µg g^{-1}) in different experimental plots (±SE)

Experimental plots	*Autumn*	*Winter*	*Spring*	*Rainy*	*Autumn*
Myrica	7.80±	10.61±	8.43±	3.45±	6.56±
	0.54	1.49	0.51	0.43	1.25
Rhododendron	8.76±	14.93±	13.71±	8.33±	9.18±
	0.76	1.17	2.80	2.25	0.6
Neolitsea	17.24±	22.28±	17.50±	11.39±	17.10±
	1.89	1.11	0.74	1.59	1.69
Mixed	18.10±	23.43±	19.63±	8.23±	16.68±
	2.78	3.55	3.97	0.95	4.07

Table 8.4
Two-way ANOVA showing effects of seasons and experimental plots on soil microbial biomass carbon (MBC µg g^{-1}), microbial biomass nitrogen (MBN µg g^{-1}) and microbial biomass phosphorus (MBP µg g^{-1})

Parameters	*Source of variance*	*Degrees of freedom*	*Calculated F value*	*Tabulated F value*	*Significance level*
MBC	Seasons	4	49.43	4.6	<0.05
	Plots	3	94.11	5.4	<0.05
MBN	Seasons	4	75.10	4.6	<0.05
	Plots	3	15.28	5.4	<0.05
MBP	Seasons	4	41.16	4.6	<0.05
	Plots	3	90.52	5.4	<0.05

Table 8.5
Mean soil microbial biomass –carbon (MBC µg g^{-1}), –nitrogen (MBN µg g^{-1}) and –phosphorus (MBP µg g^{-1}) and their contribution (%) to soil organic carbon (SOC) and total nitrogen (TKN) in different experimental plots (each value is a mean of 45 replicates across 5 seasons)

Experimental plots	*MBC*	*MBC/SO ratio %*	*MBN ratio*	*MBN/ TKN ratio (%)*	*MBP*
Myrica	386.63[a]	1.48	26.52	0.46	7.37
Rhododendron	700.95	2.26	34.23[a]	0.44	10.98
Neolitsea	521.64	1.83	36.42[a, b]	0.45	17.10[a]
Mixed	390.19[a]	1.37	41.85[b]	0.47	17.21[a]
LSD (p<0.05)	55.68		5.93		1.86

[a,b] Values with similar superscripts in the column are not significant

Available inorganic nitrogen (NH_4^+– N + NO_3^-–N)

Ammonium nitrogen concentration (NH_4^+– N)

The NH_4^+– N concentration was significantly ($p<0.05$) high in *Rhododendron* plot than other three plots. The difference between other three plots was not significant. The average NH_4^+–N values ranged from 10.22 to 11.40 µg g^{-1} (Table 8.7). Marked seasonality was observed in all the plots with high concentration recorded in dry period (13 –17 µg g^{-1}) and low during wet period (4 –7 µg g^{-1}) (Figure 8.1).

Nitrate nitrogen concentration (NO_3^-–N)

The NO_3^-–N concentration varies from 7.24 – 8.63 µg g^{-1} (Table 8.7). The values did not differ significantly ($p<0.05$) between *Rhododendron* and *Neolitsea* plots, and Mixed and *Neolitsea* plots. The value was significantly low in *Myrica* plots. The seasonal pattern was similar to NH_4^+– N (Figure 8.2).

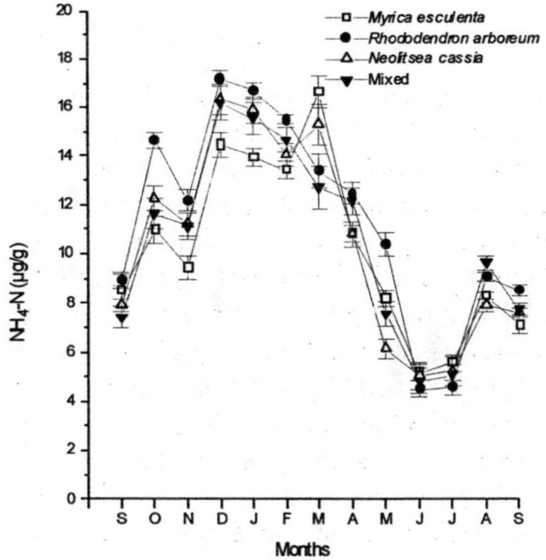

Figure 8.1 Variation in ammonium nitrogen (NH_4–N) in surface soil layer (0–10 cm) in different experimental plots

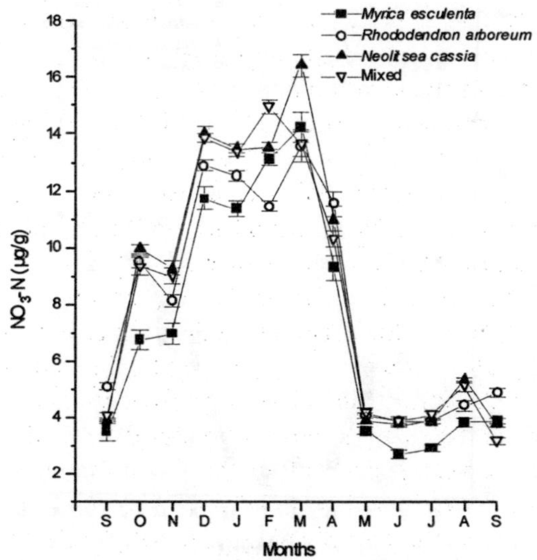

Figure 8.2 Variation in nitrate nitrogen (NO_3–N) in surface soil layer (0–10 cm) in different experimental plots

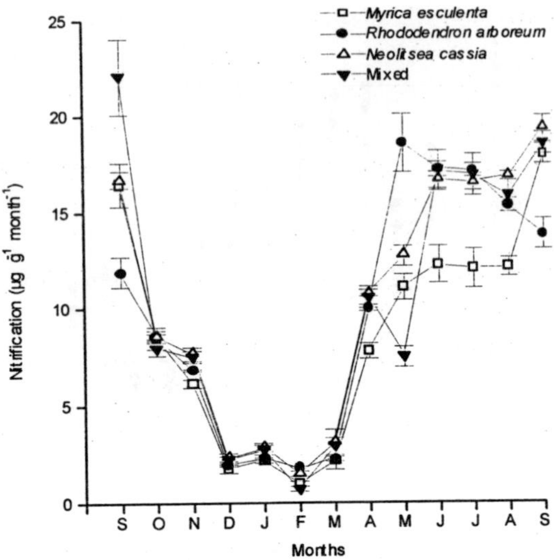

Figure 8.3 Net nitrification rate in surface soil layer (0–10 cm) of experimental plots

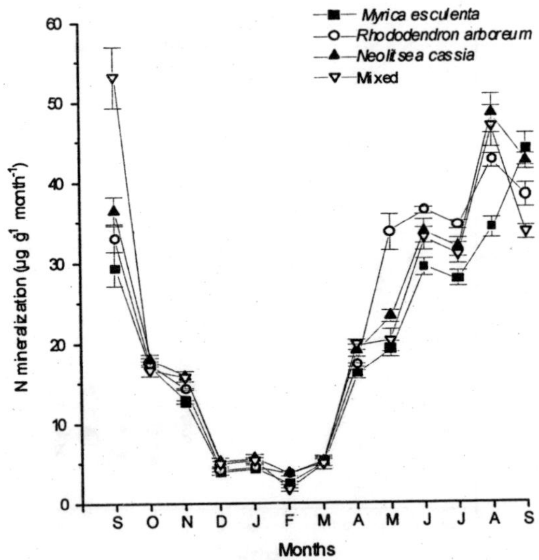

Figure 8.4 Net N mineralization rates in surface soil layer (0–10 cm) of experimental plots

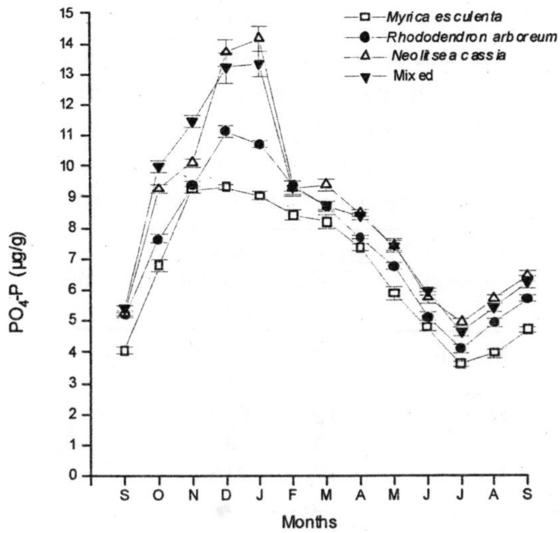

Figure 8.5 Variation in inorganic phosphorus (PO_4–P) in surface soil layer (0–10 cm) in experimental plots

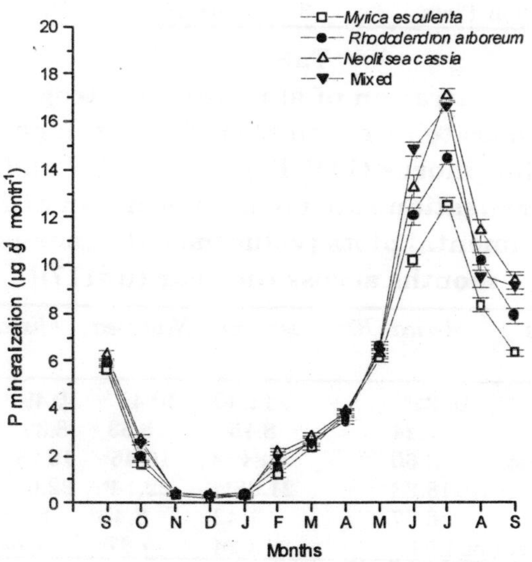

Figure 8.6 Net P mineralization rate in surface soil layer (0–10 cm) of experimental plots

Table 8.6

Two way ANOVA showing the effects of months and different experimental plots on ammonium nitrogen (NH_4^+–N, µg g^{-1}), nitrate nitrogen (NO_3^-–N, µg g^{-1}), phosphate phosphorus (PO_4^{3-}–P, µg g^{-1}) and N and P mineralization rate (µg g^{-1}month^{-1})

Parameters	*Source of variation*	*Degrees of freedom*	*Calculated F value*	*Tabulated F value*	*Significance Level (P)*
NH_4^+–N	Months	12	197.67	2.7	<0.001
	Plots	3	12.01	5.4	<0.001
NO_3^-–N	Months	12	672.26	2.7	<0.001
	Plots	3	43.63	5.4	<0.001
Nitrification	Months	12	218.59	2.7	<0.001
	Plots	3	12.68	5.4	<0.001
N	Months	12	315.59	2.7	<0.001
mineralization	Plots	3	12.31	5.4	<0.001
PO_4^{3-}–P	Months	12	372.49	2.7	<0.001
	Plots	3	149.23	5.4	<0.001
P	Months	12	981.66	2.7	<0.001
mineralization	Plots	3	48.76	5.4	<0.001

Table 8.7

Mean concentration of ammonium nitrogen (NH_4^+–N, µg g^{-1}), nitrate nitrogen (NO_3^-–N, µg g^{-1}), phosphate phosphorus (PO_4^{3-}–P, µg g^{-1}) and N and P mineralization rate (µg g^{-1}month^{-1}) in different experimental plots [values are the means of 13 months across the year (n=117)]

Parameters	*Myrica*	*Rhododendron*	*Neolitsea*	*Mixed*	*LSD (p<0.001)*
NH_4^+–N	10.22[a,b]	11.40	10.45 [b,c]	10.49 [a,c]	0.55
NO_3^-–N	7.24	8.15 [a]	8.63 [b]	8.39 [a,b]	0.34
Nitrification	8.60	9.84 [a,b]	10.45[b,c]	10.22[a,c]	0.85
N mineralization	18.83	21.88[a,b]	22.14[b,c]	22.01[a,c]	1.66
PO_4^{3-}–P	6.57	7.42	8.45[a]	8.42[a]	0.27
P mineralization	4.54	5.24	5.87[a]	5.74[a]	0.32

[a,b,c] Values with similar superscript alphabets a,b and c in the columns are not significant.

Nitrification

The mean nitrification rate ranged from 8.60 – 10.45 µg $g^{-1}month^{-1}$ though did not vary significantly ($p<0.001$) between *Rhododendron, Neolitsea* and Mixed plots, but *Myrica* plot (8.60 µg $g^{-1}month^{-1}$) recorded lowest nitrification rate (Table 8.7).

ANOVA of the result showed a marked ($p<0.001$) difference in the nitrification rate across the months (Table 8.6). In all the experimental plots higher values were recorded during September (16 – 22 µg $g^{-1}month^{-1}$) except for *Rhododendron* plot, and lower values during February (0.74 – 1.8 µg $g^{-1}month^{-1}$) (Figure 8.3).

Net N mineralization

Net N mineralization was significantly ($p<0.001$) affected by tree species ranging from 18.83 – 22.14 µg $g^{-1}month^{-1}$. Rate of net nitrification and N mineralization was low in *Myrica* plot and high under *Rhododendron, Neolitsea* and Mixed plots (Table 8.7).

The seasonal pattern of N mineralization and nitrification was similar in all plots; being maximum in the rainy (29 – 53 µg $g^{-1}month^{-1}$) and minimum in the winter season (1.65 – 3.60 µg $g^{-1}month^{-1}$) (Figure 8.4).

Inorganic phosphorus (PO_4^{3-}– P)

Two way ANOVA revealed significant ($p<0.001$) difference in phosphate phosphorus (PO_4 - P) concentration between the months and experimental plots (Table 8.6). Based on the PO_4–P concentration the experimental plots can be arranged in the order: *Neolitsea* ≥ Mixed > *Rhododendron* > *Myrica* (Table 8.7). Its seasonal changes were similar to inorganic nitrogen (NH_4^+–N and NO_3^-–N) in all the plots (Figure 8.5). Highest values were recorded during the dry winter period (9 – 14 µg $g^{-1}month^{-1}$) and lowest during the wet rainy period (3.62 – 4.92 µg $g^{-1}month^{-1}$).

Net P mineralization

The net P mineralization rate ranged from 4.54 – 5.87 $\mu g\ g^{-1} month^{-1}$. Based on the mean P mineralization rate the experimental plots may be arranged in the following order: *Neolitsea* ≥ Mixed > *Rhododendron* > *Myrica* (Table 8.7).

The seasonal pattern of P mineralization was similar to N mineralization, being maximum in the rainy (12.51 – 17.09 $\mu g\ g^{-1} month^{-1}$) and minimum in the winter (0.24 – 0.36 $\mu g\ g^{-1} month^{-1}$) season in all the plots (Figure 8.6).

Discussion

Peak microbial biomass C, N and P during winter and lowest values during rainy season recorded in the present study is similar to the findings of Maithani (1996), Upadhaya (2002) and Upadhaya *et al.* (2006) in the subtropical forest. The drop in microbial biomass in the beginning of the rainy season has been attributed to lysis and microbiovory, which are favoured by high temperature and soil moisture conditions of rainy season. This might be responsible for the release of organically bound nutrients in microbial biomass and low microbial biomass during this season. When soil moisture level and temperature was low during winter season due to slow turn over microbial biomass peaked during this season leading to greater nutrient retention in its biomass. This is evident from a strong negative correlation observed between SMC and ST and MBC, MBN and MBP (Table 8.8).

The concentration of MBC obtained in the present study (257.9 – 922.2 $\mu g\ g^{-1}$) is within the reported range (61 – 2,000 $\mu g\ g^{-1}$) for various temperate and tropical forest soils (Vance *et al.* 1987a, Henrot and Robertson 1994, Diaz-Ravina *et al.* 1995). Maximum MBC in *Rhododendron* plots as compared to the other plots clearly show the effect of tree species which added greater amount of organic matter and nutrients to soil that might have favoured the growth of microbial population and accumulation of microbial biomass. A significant positive relationship between MBC and soil organic carbon (r= 0.35, p= 0.001) in the present study as well as those of Upadhaya (2002) and Arunachalam *et al.* (1996) provide support to the hypothesis that an increase in organic matter content leads to greater microbial products. Diaz-Ravina *et al.* (1988) have reported that soil with low organic C usually has less microbial biomass and vice versa. Low soil organic carbon in Mixed and *Myrica* plots could explain the low MBC. Bauhas *et al.* (1998) studied the effect of tree species on soil microbial biomass with concentrations of MBC and MBN, and found lower values beneath conifers than deciduous tree species. This is attributed to the differences in foliage litter quality as microbial biomass decreased with increasing C/N or lignin/N ratios. Contrary to this, MBC was positively correlated with lignin, C/N and lignin/N ratios.

The contribution of MBC to SOC in the present study (1.37 – 2.26%) is well within the range reported from other tropical forest (1.5 – 5.3%; Theng *et al.* 1989 and Luizao *et al.* 1992), tropical dry deciduous forest (1.6 – 3.6%; Srivastava and Singh 1989), temperate forest soils (1.8 – 2.9%; Vance *et al.* 1987a), pinewood and oakwood forests, (0.5 – 2%; Diaz-Ravina *et al.* 1995).

The concentration of MBN (21.1 – 89.2 $\mu g\ g^{-1}$) in the present study was lower than that of soil of evergreen forest (42 – 242 $\mu g\ g^{-1}$; Martikainen and Palojarvi 1990), pinewood and oakwood forests (42 – 191 $\mu g\ g^{-1}$; Diaz-Ravina *et al.* 1995). However, it was comparable to the values reported from subtropical forest regrowth (37.8 – 123.9 $\mu g\ g^{-1}$; Maithani *et al.* 1996) and tropical forest (27 – 93 $\mu g\ g^{-1}$; Barbhuiya 2006) of this region.

The observed difference in concentration of MBN between the experimental plots was related to soil pH and TKN (Table 8.8). Therefore, higher concentration of MBN in Mixed plot could be attributable to the higher TKN, pH and lower soil C/N. Although the resource quality of litter in Mixed plot was better, a relationship between litter quality (lignin, C/N and lignin/N ratios) and MBN was weak (Table 8.8). The contribution of MBN to TKN was much lower (0.44 – 0.47%) compared to a range of forest soils (3.4 – 5.9%; Martikainen and Palojarvi 1990), pinewood and oakwood forests, (1.5 – 4.5%; Diaz-Ravina *et al.*1995), subtropical forest regrowth (7.3 – 8.3%; Maithani *et al.* 1996) and disturbed humid tropical forest (1.3 – 1.7%; Barbhuiya 2006).

The MBP obtained in different experimental plots (3.45 – 23.43 μg g^{-1}) was lower compared to the reported range (5 – 67 μg g^{-1}) for woodland soils (Brookes *et al.* 1984). However, the values were close to dry tropical ecosystems (9 – 28 μg g^{-1}; Srivastava 1992). The higher concentration of MBP in Mixed and *Neolitsea* plots could be due to the higher soil available P and pH as evident from the positive correlation between them (Table 8.8). In this case, a strong correlation between litter quality (lignin, C/N and lignin/N ratios) and MBP were observed (Table 8.8). Greater concentrations of microbial biomass is generally found in soils of higher soil organic matter and pH (Blagodatskaya and Anderson 1998, Bååth and Anderson 2003) and that soil pH appears to influence microbial community composition (Bååth and Anderson 2003, Malmivaara–Lämsä and Fritze 2003). This is supported by the strong correlation between soil chemical properties and soil microbial biomass C, N and P (Table 8.8).

Thus, differences in the amount and quality of soil organic matter and soil pH due to change in species composition in the plots led to differences in microbial biomass.

Table 8.8
Relationship between MBC, MBN and MBP (μg g⁻¹) and soil physico–chemical properties and litter quality in the experimental plots

Variable	*Regression Equation*	*Degrees of freedom*	*Correlation co–efficient (r)*	*P level*
1	*2*	*3*	*4*	*5*
MBC vs. soil chemical properties				
SOC	Y= –9.24 + 176.72X	179	0.35*	<0.001
TKN	Y= 381.93 + 152.92X	179	0.14*	<0.05
Av.P	Y= 2.95 + 0.002X	179	0.27*	<0.001
C:N	Y= 537.26 – 0.41X	179	–0.11	0.14
pH	Y= –763.31+ 282.22X	179	0.44*	<0.001
vs. soil physical properties				
ST	Y= 994.95 – 31.23X	179	–0.54*	<0.001
SMC	Y= 731.93 – 5.11X	179	–0.27*	<0.001
vs. litter quality				
N	Y= 887.47 – 279.03 X	179	–0.41*	<0.001
P	Y= 507.72 – 148.18X	179	–0.01	0.87
C/N	Y= 163.27 + 9.58X	179	0.41*	<0.001
Lignin	Y= 249.95 + 9.23X	179	0.35*	<0.001
MBN vs. soil chemical properties				
SOC	Y= 14.86 + 7.00X	179	0.15*	<0.05
TKN	Y= 7.88 + 35.22X	179	0.35*	<0.01
Av.P	Y= 25.54 + 2.43X	179	0.18	0.02

(Contd...)

1	*2*	*3*	*4*	*5*
C:N	Y= 57.22 – 5.64X	179	– 0.29*	<0.001
pH	Y= –199.55 + 52.35X	179	0.85*	<0.001
vs. soil physical properties				
ST	Y= 101.51 – 4.21X	179	–0.76*	<0.001
SMC	Y= 79.03 – 0.97X	179	–0.56*	<0.001
vs. litter quality				
N	Y= 23.02 + 8.44X	179	0.13	0.07
P	Y= 16.59 + 341.59X	179	0.27*	<0.001
C/N	Y= 44.07 – 0.26X	179	–0.11	0.10
Lignin	Y= 42.77 – 0.29X	179	–0.12	0.10
MBP vs. soil chemical properties				
SOC	Y= 2.66 + 0.02X	179	0.27*	<0.001
TKN	Y= 1.07 + 15.69X	179	0.46*	<0.001
Av.P	Y= 3.32 + 2.52X	179	0.55*	<0.001
C:N	Y= 21.38 – 2.08X	179	– 0.32*	<0.001
pH	Y= –41.77+ 12.27X	179	0.59*	<0.001
vs. soil physical properties				
ST	Y= 28.12 – 0.94X	179	–0.50*	<0.001
SMC	Y= 17.13 – 0.08X	179	–0.15*	<0.001
vs. litter quality				
N	Y= –2.65 + 11.39X	179	0.52*	<0.001
P	Y= –0.97 + 265.96X	179	0.63*	<0.001
C/N	Y= 26.10 – 0.36X	179	–0.48*	<0.001
Lignin	Y= 24.16 – 0.40X	179	–0.48*	<0.001

Table 8.9
Relationships between nitrification, N and P mineralization (μg g^{-1} $month^{-1}$) and soil physico–chemical properties, litter quality and microbial biomass in the experimental plots (n= 36)

Parameters	*Regression Equation*	*Correlation co-efficient (r)*	*Significance level (p)*
1	*2*	*3*	*4*
Nitrification vs. soil physical properties			
ST	Y= 26.31 – 1.07X	–0.80*	<0.001
SMC	Y= 4.19 + 0.13X	0.69*	<0.001
vs. soil properties			
pH	Y= –16.31 + 5.74X	0.75*	<0.001
C/N	Y= 14.64 – 1.26X	–0.79*	<0.001
SOC	Y= 6.32 + 1.20X	0.35*	<0.05
TKN	Y= 5.66 + 5.34X	0.78*	<0.001
Av. P	Y= 7.11 + 0.68X	0.78*	<0.001
vs. litter chemical quality			
N	Y= 8.00 + 1.28X	0.42*	<0.01
P	Y= 7.50 + 42.84X	0.73*	<0.001
C/N	Y= 11.14 – 0.03X	–0.36*	<0.05
Lignin	Y= 11.13 – 0.05X	–0.42*	<0.05
vs. MBN	Y= 7.23 + 0.07X	0.59*	<0.001
N mineralization vs. soil physical properties			
ST	Y= 52.30 – 2.02X	–0.79*	<0.001
SMC	Y= 10.13 + 0.26X	0.71*	<0.001

(Contd...)

1	*2*	*3*	*4*
vs. soil chemical properties			
pH	Y= –30.62 + 11.42X	0.78*	<0.001
C/N	Y= 30.05 – 2.31X	–0.76*	<0.001
SOC	Y= 12.16 + 3.14X	0.48*	<0.05
TKN	Y= 13.12 + 10.51X	0.81*	<0.001
Av. P	Y= 16.25 + 1.27X	0.76*	<0.001
vs. litter quality			
N	Y=18.80 + 1.73X	0.30	0.07
P	Y= 17.35 + 72.71X	0.65*	<0.001
C/N	Y= 23.00 – 0.05X	–0.25	0.13
Lignin	Y= 22.37 – 0.05X	–0.24	0.15
vs. MBN	Y= 16.63 + 0.13X	0.56*	<0.001
P mineralization vs. soil physical properties			
ST	Y= 17.36 – 1.07X	–0.92*	<0.001
SMC	Y= 2.05 + 0.08X	0.64*	<0.001
vs. soil chemical properties			
pH	Y= –12.22 + 3.87X	0.80*	<0.001
C/N	Y= 8.66 – 0.86X	–0.86*	<0.001
SOC	Y= 4.37 + 0.34X	0.15	0.37
TKN	Y= 2.86 + 3.22X	0.75*	<0.001
Av. P	Y= 3.60 + 0.45X	0.80*	<0.001
vs. litter quality			
N	Y= 3.68 + 1.19X	0.61*	<0.001
P	Y= 3.51 + 34.49X	0.92*	<0.001
C/N	Y= 6.77 – 0.04X	–0.61*	<0.001
Lignin	Y= 6.49 – 0.04X	–0.57*	<0.001
vs. MBP	Y= 4.10 + 0.09X	0.79*	<0.001

Table 8.10

Results of multiple regression analysis for effect of soil physico-chemical properties, soil microbial biomass and litter quality on nitrification, N and P mineralization

	Dependent variables	*No. of cases*	R^2	*F*	*df*	*Intercept*	*β*
1	*2*	*3*	*4*	*5*	*6*	*7*	*8*
Soil physical properties	Nitrification	36	0.68	35.20	(2,33)	20.90	ST= -0.64* SMC= 0.24
	N mineralization	36	0.68	35.52	(2,33)	39.18	ST= -0.58* SMC= .31*
	P mineralization	36	0.85	97.13	(2,33)	17.57	ST= -0.93* SMC=-0.01
Soil chemical properties	Nitrification	36	0.73	20.82	(4,31)	0.84	pH= 0.19 SOC= -0.14 TKN= 0.45* Av.P= 0.35*
	N mineralization	36	0.75	22.76	(4,31)	-9.22	pH= 0.37* SOC= 0.09 TKN= 0.31 Av.P= 0.22
	P mineralization	36	0.83	38.94	(4,31)	0.12	pH= 0.24 SOC= -0.40*

(Contd...)

1	*2*	*3*	*4*	*5*	*6*	*7*	*8*
							TKN= 0.48* Av.P= 0.44*
Soil microbial biomass	Nitrification	36	0.73	28.18	(3,32)	6.97	MBC= 0.29* MBN= -0.04 MBP= 0.85*
	N mineralization	36	0.75	31.73	(3,32)	15.68	MBC= 0.41* MBN= -0.12 MBP= 0.88*
	P mineralization	36	0.67	21.29	(3,32)	3.64	MBC= 0.12 MBN= 0.12 MBP= 0.72*
Litter quality	Nitrification	36	0.80	30.14	(4,31)	-34.48	N= 5.08* P= 0.96* C/N= 4.92* Lignin= 0.55*
	N mineralization	36	0.76	24.09	(4,31)	-73.73	N= 5.70* P= 0.99* C/N= 5.33* Lignin= 0.96*
	P mineralization	36	0.87	54.15	(4,31)	4.34	N= -0.29 P= 1.05* C/N= -0.03* Lignin= -0.11

Available nutrients

Variation of available nutrient pool (inorganic N and P) in soil is dependent on several factors such as mineralization rates, uptake by plants and microbes, and losses through soil erosion, leaching, run-off and denitrification. The higher concentration in soil nutrients during dry winter period may be due to reduced uptake by plants, minimal leaching losses and their immobilization in microbial biomass. Conversely, higher nutrient uptake by vegetation, lower immobilization and increased leaching and runoff losses were responsible for smaller nutrient pool during wet season. Schmitt and Randall (1994) suggested that lower nitrate-N during rainy season could be because of NO_3^- losses via leaching and denitrification. Singh *et al.* (1991) reported that plant uptake is high during wet period and immobilization in microbial biomass is low compared to dry period.

Nitrification, N and P mineralization rates

The significant difference in nitrification, N and P mineralization rates observed between the experimental plots is attributable largely to the influences of the tree species on the soil environment since they can determine the biological, chemical and physical conditions in the soils (Binkley and Giardina 1998, Priha and Smolander 1999, Augusto *et al.* 2002, Brüggerman *et al.* 2005). The composition of the leaf litters especially their C/N ratio and lignin/N ratio govern the soil microbial processes involved in decomposition and transformation of C, N and P containing compounds (Gower and Son 1992, Stump and Binkley 1993, Scott and Binkley 1997). Lignin plays an important role in N transformation, as it is converted preferentially into persistent humic substances during the process of humification, thereby additionally binding inorganic nitrogen compounds and making them unavailable for plants and microbes (Thomas and Prescott 2000). Litters with high ratios of lignin/N tend to decompose slowly (Melillo *et al.* 1982) and soils produced by those litters have been reported to have low N mineralization rates (Scott and Binkley 1997). Contrary to this, strong correlations between (N, lignin, C/N ratio) and soil N mineralization rates were not observed in the present study. Strong correlations between soil physico-chemical properties, soil microbial biomass and litter quality and nitrification and mineralization rates observed in the present study indicate that litter quality of the tree species alone do not determine the mineralization rate, but other factors on the forest floor such as microbial biomass and soil nutrient status also play important role in determining the rate of these soil biological processes (Table 8.10).

Further, a strong correlation between soil moisture content and soil temperature and nitrification, N and P mineralization rates suggests that differences in soil physical properties brought about through a change in species composition might be one of the potential causes for the differences in nitrification, N and P mineralization rates between the plots. Variation in N and P transformation in the plots was related to MBN and MBP as both were positively correlated with each other.

In general, tree species influence at least in the upper layers of the forest soil due to differences in litter composition (Priha and Smolander 1999). Change in soil pH affects soil C and N turnover, as the pH plays a crucial role in soil microbial processes (Persson and Wiren 1993). Wang *et al.* (2006) have reported that soil alkaline phosphatase activity, arylsulphatase activity, nitrification potential and respiration are significantly reduced after acidification of soil.

The high nitrification, net N and P mineralization under *Neolitsea* and Mixed plots had high pH, TKN, Av.P, extractable inorganic P, moderate levels of SOC and inorganic N and lowest C/N ratio. These soil parameters had low values in *Rhododendron* plots as compared to *Neolitsea* and Mixed plots and lowest in *Myrica* plots. Thus tree species exerted influence on soil N and P transformation processes primarily through change in the quantity and quality of soil organic matter. The differences among the plots suggest that N and P transformation in the forest floor vary from place to place depending on the distribution pattern of dominant trees in the patch.

9

General Discussion

The humid subtropical forest ecosystem in Meghalaya is a closed canopy forest characterized by high diversity of vascular pants, complex community organization and high spatial heterogeneity in species distribution and forest microenvironment. The dominant tree species in the forest show distinct patchy distribution depending on the availability of favourable microenvironment for successful establishment of their seedlings on the forest floor.

Vegetation type, community structure and canopy closure influence the microclimate on the forest floor (Martius *et al.* 2004, Upadhaya 2002, Raich and Tufekciouglu 2000), while tree species influence soil properties and biogeochemical cycles through input of detrital materials in the form of litter and fine roots. Soil microbes associated with different tree species often have variable amounts of biomass (Bauhas *et al.* 1998, Templer *et al.* 2003), and rates of decomposition of organic matter, nitrification (Finzi *et al.* 1998a, Menyailo *et al.* 2003, Brüggemann *et al.* 2005), and mineralization (Menyailo *et al.* 2003, Brüggemann *et al.* 2005).

Effect of tree species on microclimate

There was a marked change in microclimatic parameters

in different plots in the forest understorey. A decrease in light intensity and air temperature and an increase in relative humidity from *Myrica* plot to Mixed plot were related to a gradual increase in canopy cover from *Myrica* plots (73%) to *Rhododendron* plots (79%), *Neolitsea* and Mixed plots (81%). The microclimatic variables in *Neolitsea* and Mixed plots were similar due to presence of more common species and closeness of the plots. Dela Cruz and Luna (1994), Luna *et al.* (1999), Raich and Tufekciouglu (2000), Rijkers *et al.* (2000), Upadhaya (2002), Martius *et al.* (2004) and Brüggemann *et al.* (2005) have found similar results in which tree composition modifies the forest microclimate. Leaf size, their display, phenology as well as architecture of tree species also play an important role in affecting the microclimatic condition (Meinzer and Goldstein 1996). Dela Cruz and Luna (1994) and Luna *et al.* (1999) reported that tree stands modify the microclimate in terms of reduced air and surface soil temperature, increased relative humidity and reduced irradiance compared to grasslands. Kozlowski and Pallardy (1997) reported that air temperature affects growth and development of woody plants directly by inducing injury and indirectly by influencing physiological processes that affect yield and quality of fruits and seeds. Brüggemann *et al.* (2005) suggested that the soil surfaces under more translucent tree species, such as pine, oak and larch, receive more light and warm up more during the vegetation period than the soils beneath shadier tree species, such as beech and spruce. These differences in the microclimate of the stands could be one of the potential causes for species-specific differences in soil properties.

Effect of tree species on soil physical properties

Canopy openness has a strong effect on the soil temperature due to greater penetration of radiant energy as observed under *Myrica* plots, which were warmer than the other three plots. Similarly, a close relationship between soil temperature and radiant energy input at the soil surface was reported by Balisky and Burton (1993). The soil moisture content depends on the amount of precipitation reaching the forest floor and is largely influenced by the morphology of the tree species. The lower soil moisture content as observed in *Myrica* plots could be the result of high evaporation from the soil owing to openness of canopy and low water retention due to high proportion of sand. A marked increased in soil moisture content in *Rhododendron* plots could be attributed to a dense canopy cover, greater accumulation of litter on the forest floor and markedly greater proportion of clay in soil. All these check evaporation losses on one hand and help in moisture retention on the other.

Effect of tree species on soil chemical properties

Studies of Konova (1966) and Finzi *et al.* (1998b) provided ample proof that relatively thick forest floor and slower rates of litter decomposition increases the quantity of organic acids thereby lowering the soil pH. This could be probably the reason for high soil acidity in *Myrica* plot than the other three plots. The high soil organic carbon content in *Rhododendron* plots was related to slower decay rate and therefore greater accumulation of litter and fine roots. High concentration of TKN and Av. P in soils of Mixed and *Neolitsea* plots respectively could be due to greater amount of nutrient input to soil through litter and fine roots (Chapter 7). The litter quality (low C/N or lignin/N ratio) in these plots was also good, which lead to faster release of nutrients through rapid decomposition (Melillo *et al.* 1982, Prescott *et al.* 1993, Stump and Binkley 1993, Prescott 1995). Subtle differences in the rate of litter decomposition spanning temporal scales of decades to centuries can lead to large differences in organic matter accumulation and the C and N content of soils (Parton *et al.* 1987). *Myrica esculenta* being N-fixing species, showed low soil organic matter, TKN and Av. P contents due to poor litter quality (high C/N or lignin/N ratio) and less favourable microclimatic condition (high soil temperature or low soil moisture content) for its decomposition. Dudley *et al.* (1996) have also reported that the nitrogen fixed by *Myrica pensylvanica* in coastal heathland ecosystem did not add to the soil nitrogen pool. Further, the low concentration of nitrogen in the soil under *Myrica* could also be the result of leaching because of sandy nature of the soil.

Effect of tree species on soil biological properties

Microbial biomass and their activity are influenced by the resource quality of litter, and texture, organic matter and nutrient content of soil. High MBC in *Rhododendron* plots as compared to the other plots could be the result of greater input of organic matter and nutrients through litter and fine roots, which might have favoured the growth of microbial population and greater microbial biomass. This is evident from significant positive correlation between MBC and SOC ($r= 0.35$, $p= 0.001$). Similar results obtained by Upadhaya (2002) and Arunachalam *et al.* (1996) was attributed to an increase in organic matter content in soil due to greater accumulation of plant derived organic matter and microbial products. Soil with low organic C usually has less microbial biomass and vice versa (Diaz-Ravina *et al.* 1988). Low soil organic carbon in Mixed and *Myrica* plot could well explain the low MBC. Bauhas *et al.* (1998) studied the effect of tree species on soil microbial biomass and reported that concentrations of MBC and MBN was lower beneath conifers than under deciduous tree species, probably due to differences in foliage litter quality as microbial biomass decrease with increasing C/N or lignin/N ratios.

The observed difference in concentration of MBN between the experimental plots was also related to TKN ($r= 0.35$; $p<0.01$). Besides TKN, higher MBN and MBP in Mixed and *Neolitsea* plots could be attributable to greater availability of P, high soil pH and lower C/N of litter that favour growth of the microbes on the forest floor as is evident from the positive correlation between MBP and soil parameters and litter quality (Table 8.8). Thus differences in the quantity and quality of soil organic matter and soil pH due to change in species composition in the plots was responsible for the differences in microbial biomass, since greater concentrations of microbial biomass are generally found in soils with higher soil organic matter and high pH (Blagodatskaya and Anderson 1998, Bååth and Anderson 2003). Soil pH are known to influence microbial community composition too (Bååth and Anderson 2003, Malmivaara-Lämsä and Fritze 2003).

Pool of inorganic N and P in soil is influenced by three main processes, viz, their mineralization rates, uptake by plants and microbes, and losses through soil erosion, leaching, run off and denitrification (in case of N). Smaller pool of inorganic N and P in *Myrica* plot could be due to their greater losses through leaching and runoff on account of sandy nature of the soil and lower organic matter and microbial biomass that help in retention of NH_4^+–N, NO_3^-–N and PO_4^{3-}–P. The soil pH plays an important role in the availability of NH_3, which decreases exponentially with decreasing pH (De Boer and Kowalchuk 2001). Growth of nitrifiers is also known to be affected by low pH, and moisture stress (Grant 1994). These factors might be at work in *Myrica* plot. Greater inorganic N and P pool in soil of other three plots was associated with higher soil organic matter, pH, and moisture level in soil.

The significant differences in nitrification, N and P mineralization rates observed between the experimental plots might be attributable largely to the influences of the tree species on the soil environment since trees determine the biological, chemical and physical conditions of the soils underneath (Binkley and Giardina 1998, Priha and Smolander 1999, Augusto *et al.* 2002, Brüggeman *et al.*

2005). The composition of the leaf litter especially the C/N ratio and lignin/N ratio are important factors governing the soil microbial processes involved in decomposition and transformation of C, N and P containing compounds (Gower and Son 1992, Stump and Binkley 1993, Scott and Binkley 1997). Lignin plays an important role in N transformation, as it is converted preferentially into persistent humic substances during the process of humification, thereby additionally binding inorganic N compounds and making them unavailable for plants and microbes (Thomas and Prescott 2000). Litters with high ratios of lignin/N tend to decompose slowly (Melillo *et al.* 1982) and soils produced by those litters have been reported to have low N mineralization rates (Scott and Binkley 1997). Contrary to this, strong correlations between N, lignin and C/N ratio and soil N mineralization rates were not observed in the present study. Strong correlations between soil physico-chemical properties, soil microbial biomass, litter quality and nitrification and mineralization rates observed in the present study indicates that the litter quality alone does not determine the mineralization rate, but other factors like forest floor microenvironment; microbial biomass and soil nutrient status also play an important role (Table 8.10).

The difference in MBN and MBP was related to N and P mineralization rate respectively. In general, tree species in the plots can have a significant influence on pH at least in the upper layers of the forest soil due to differences in litter composition (Priha and Smolander 1999). As the pH has crucial effects on soil microbial processes (Persson and Wiren 1993) it can alter turnover of soil C and N. Wang *et al.* (2006) reported that soil alkaline phosphatase activity, arylsulphatase activity, nitrification potential and respiration were significantly reduced after acidification of soil.

The high nitrification, net N and P mineralization occurred in *Neolitsea* and Mixed plots where soil had high pH, TKN,

Av.P, extractable inorganic P, intermediate level of SOC and inorganic N and lowest value of C/N ratio. The values of these soil parameters in *Rhododendron* plots were in between *Neolitsea* and Mixed plots and *Myrica* plots. These differences between the plots suggest that N and P transformation on the forest floor is likely to be patchy and is dependent on the dominant trees in the patch.

Effect of tree species on accumulation, production and decomposition of tree litter

Facelli and Pickett (1991) reported that species composition is an important factor that determines litter production within the same climate range. This seems to be true even at a micro level within the forest community where species show distinct patchy distribution. Significantly ($p<0.05$) high litterfall in *Rhododendron* plots as compared to other experimental plots could be partly due to the inherent characteristics of the tree species, their density and diverse responses of species to different environmental factors (Issac and Nair 2006, Yang *et al.* 2005, George and Kumar 1998).

The overall similar seasonal pattern of litterfall in all the plots in spite of difference in species composition indicates strong overriding control of climatic factors on this process. In the present study, the peak litterfall observed in March (spring season) is similar to other's observation made in evergreen broadleaved forest (Yang *et al.* 2004a, Arunachalam 1996, Khiewtam and Ramakrishnan 1993). A small peak in *Myrica, Rhododendron* and *Neolitsea* plots in August (rainy season) is attributed to the impact of high rainfall during that month.

The litter accumulation in the experimental plots was inversely related to its turnover rate. This finding is consistent with the results of Vogt *et al.* (1986), who assigned rapid decomposition of litter as an important cause of lower litter accumulation on the forest floor of wet tropical forest. Arul

Pargasan and Parthasarathy (2005) also reported that the significant differences in total litter accumulation between two tropical dry evergreen forest sites on the Coromandel coast of south India, was due to differences in temperature, soil moisture and decomposition rates besides vegetation variables. The greater accumulation of litter in *Rhododendron* plots was due to its high density as evident by a significant positive correlation between tree density and litter mass ($Y= -8.42 + 0.004X$, $r= 0.61$, $p<0.05$).

The faster weight loss of mixed leaf litter (47 – 71%) during 400 days than the single species leaf litter (44 – 62%) could be attributed to its high N and low lignin concentration. It is hypothesized that litter mixtures decompose faster than expected when the mixture contains litter types with different N concentration. This is in agreement with the findings of the study of Hector *et al.* (2000) who found enhanced decomposition by synergistic effects of litter mixing. Conn and Dighton (2000) reported that mass loss was enhanced when oak litter was present in pine litter. Salamanca *et al.* (1998) found that the decomposition of mixed litter of two species was faster than predicted from single species litter bags. Increase in decomposition with the increase in litter diversity primarily due to synergistic, non-additive effects of litter mixing Bardgett and Shine (1999), Blair *et al.* (1990), McTiernan *et al.* (1997), Wardle *et al.* (1997b) and Chapmann *et al.* (1998) found strong, non-additive effects on decomposition rates of mixed litters that were both positive and negative. These non-additive effects have been suggested to arise in part from translocation of nutrients or inhibitory compounds in the species. Movement of nutrients from one species to another in mixtures of litter is thought to relax nutrient limitation in the decomposer community, increasing overall decomposition (Chapmann *et al.* 1988, Blair *et al.* 1990, Wardle *et al.* 1997b). These nutrients could aid the decomposition of other species in the mixture supposedly by translocation from one litter type to another by diffusion through a water film and/or active transport through the hyphae of fungi connecting two different litter types (McTiernan *et al.*1997).

Non-additive (both positive and negative) effects of litter mixing and diversity have largely been attributed to plant species traits, in particular N concentration (Swift *et al.* 1979). The present study found that the decomposition rate of the individual litter was not significantly related to their N concentration or C/N ratio. This however, does not exclude the possibility that when mixed, synergistic interactions between species of different N content might have occurred. Wardle *et al.* (1997b) showed that when litter of plants with high N status was mixed, synergistic effects on decomposition rate were observed. This is also consistent with the result of Seastedt (1984) who suggested that litter of higher quality is likely to enhance the decomposition of other litters, while poor quality litter may have negative effects. The non additive interactions have been related to other plant species traits, such as initial lignin and cellulose content (Wardle *et al.* 1997b)

All the plots exhibited a pattern characterised by a conspicuous phase of rapid decomposition of litter followed by stabilization. The faster initial phase that lasted 1–2 months (August – October) coincided with the rainy season that promotes decomposition due to favorable moisture and temperature conditions. Faster initial rates in decomposition process reflect the leaching of soluble compounds and decay of easily degradable compounds and tissues (Loranger *et al.* 2002, Swift *et al.* 1979).

Litter decomposition rates are frequently considered to be regulated by soil organisms, environmental conditions and chemical nature of the litter (Gallardo and Merino 1993). The physical environment, especially soil moisture, temperature and relative humidity are important in litter decay as these regulate the biological activity in soil. The weight loss pattern of leaf litter of dominant tree species and mixed leaf litter in different plots was positively related to soil moisture and temperature and negatively to soil pH (Table 5.10 and 5.11). Lower decomposition rates in the *Myrica* plots compared to other plots may be attributed to low soil moisture content. Zhang and Liang (1995) and Prescott *et al.* (2000) recorded lower litter decomposition rates in clear–cut areas (1 – 97 ha) or in large gaps (>15m diameter) than in small gaps and under close canopy and attributed to a higher exposure of the forest floor in the open areas to incoming radiation and wind. This seems to be true in case of *Myrica* plots.

The high moisture and organic matter content and greater microbial biomass in soil could be the reason for faster rate of decomposition of both dominant species leaf litter and mixed leaf litter in *Rhododendron* plots despite lower N and higher C/N ratio than *Myrica* plots. This explains the importance of combined effect of physical, chemical and biological properties of soil and quality and nature of litter in decomposition on the forest floor.

The annual decay constant (k) was negatively related to initial lignin, C/N and lignin/N ratios and positively to initial N concentration. Thus, higher rate of decomposition of *Neolitsea* leaf litter was due to high N and low lignin concentration and C/N ratio, while lower rate of *Myrica* leaf litter was due to lower N concentration and higher lignin concentration and C/N ratio (Table 5.10). Therefore, initial concentration of lignin seems to be the best predictor for mass losses from litter species and litter types (Sariyildiz and Anderson 2003).

Although the present study showed positive effects of increasing litter diversity on litter decomposition, the results lack the clearer positive mean response between mixed litter mass loss and species richness in the plot. In the ecosystem context, the present study provide support for the conclusion of Wardle *et al.* (1997b) that the varied nature of the effects of each species are likely to be related to its functional characteristics rather than diversity per se. Thus, the functional characteristics of component species in any ecosystem are likely to be as important as the number of species for maintaining critical ecosystem processes (Grime 1997, Hooper and Vitousek 1997). The present findings are also in agreement with Knops *et al.* (2001) suggesting that plant species richness can influence decomposition by influencing the quality of the litter and the microclimate in which the litter decomposes.

The implication of the present study is that species diversity may influence different ecosystem processes (decomposition) in different ways. There is no empirical or theoretical reason to believe that different ecological processes should all respond to diversity in a qualitatively similar way (Madritch and Cardinale 2007).

Effect of tree species on accumulation, production and decomposition of fine roots

The high fine root mass in *Rhododendron* plots than the other three plots could be due to high soil organic matter content and species diversity. This finding corroborates the study of Yang *et al.* (2004b) where higher fine root biomass was observed in natural forest with higher soil fertility, productivity and species diversity levels as compared to monoculture plantations. Persson (1983) reported that better soil conditions promote faster development of fine roots. Further a positive correlation between fine root mass and tree density ($Y = -54.55 + 0.16X$; $r = 0.85$; $p < 0.001$) in the present study corroborate the findings of Arunachalam (1996) and Visalakshi (1994) that plant density and basal area also influence the root mass.

The weight loss pattern of fine root litter in different plots on one hand was positively related to soil moisture and soil temperature and negatively to soil pH (Table 6.4) and on the other. The annual decay constant (k) was negatively related to initial lignin, C/N and Lignin/N ratios and positively to initial N concentration. Thus, the higher rate of decomposition in Mixed and *Neolitsea* plots was due to high N and low lignin concentration and C/N ratio, while lower rate of *Myrica* fine roots was due to low N and high lignin concentration and high C/N ratio (Table 6.5).

N and P input, accumulation and release through litter and fine roots

The input of N and P in soil through litter is a function of concentration and litterfall. Maximum input of N and P in Mixed plots was mainly due to resource quality of litter (high N and P concentration). This is in agreement with the findings of De Moraes *et al.* (1999) that low quality litter leads to a smaller return of mineral elements to soil. However, higher input of N in *Myrica* plots was related to high litterfall. Similarly, greater N and P accumulation in case of Mixed, *Neolitsea* and *Rhododendron* plots was related to high concentration, whereas, maximum N accumulation in *Myrica* plots mainly due to the higher litter mass. The characteristic features of the species are responsible for the differences in the nutrient content of litter between forest sites (Yang *et al.* 2005).

Concentration of N and P contributed more to the observed nutrient accumulation pattern in them. In all plots, the amount of N returned to the forest floor through fine roots was greater than P. This is consistent with the findings of Nambiar (1987), Khiewtam and Ramakrishnan (1993), Arunachalam (1996) and John (1998).

The nutrient dynamics of decomposing leaf litter generally follows three sequential phases: an initial release mainly due to leaching, net accumulation by immobilization, and net release by mineralization (Staaf and Berg 1989, Swift *et al.* 1979, Upadhaya and Singh 1989, Yamashita and Takeda 1998, Chuyong *et al.* 2002). The two nutrient elements, (N and P) examined in the present study also showed these phases in leaf litter and root litter decomposition in all the experimental plots.

Rapid rate of N release at the initial phase coincided with the rainy season (upto 60 days) mainly due to leaching of the soluble forms of N. The second phase characterized by slower rate of nutrient release from 60 – 120 days coincided with the dry winter season. This was due to immobilization and binding of N to lignin and polyphenols in the tissues (Palm and Sanchez 1990). As decay advances, decline of the element in residual litter indicate while increase indicate its immobilization. Temporary immobilization noticed in N and P suggests slow release of the nutrients from the decaying litter, which minimizes the losses from the ecosystem. Myers *et al.* (1994) reported that low quality litter materials having high C/N ratio immobilizes N at a faster rate, while the high quality litter with low C/N ratio releases nutrient at a faster rate during decomposition. Thus release of N from *Neolitsea* leaf litter, which had a C/N ratio of 27.4, was much faster compared to *Rhododendron* and *Neolitsea* that had higher C/N ratio (51.29 and 37.40 respectively). Net higher mineralization of N and P in decomposing leaf litter of *Neolitsea* was due to high resource quality of litter. Similarly, higher mineralization of N and P in decomposing mixed leaf litter and fine root litter of *Neolitsea* and Mixed plots can be attributed to good litter quality.

Effect of litter diversity on the amount of N released from decomposing litter is extremely variable. Studies in which the species diversity of litter was manipulated have resulted in increased (Blair *et al.* 1990), decreased (McTiernan *et al.* 1997) and idiosyncratic (Wardle *et al.* 1997b) patterns of N release with increasing litter diversity. The findings of the present study revealed faster N and P release from mixed leaf litter (59 – 83.5% and 54 – 69% respectively) than the single species leaf litter (52.5 – 78% and 49 – 68% respectively). This is attributed to the difference in chemical nature of the two types of litter, particularly in N, P and lignin concentration. A linear regression analysis (Table 7.7) between concentrations of pairs of nutrients during decomposition suggests that the behaviour of N and P were similar and may have influenced each other during decomposition (Xu and Hirata 2005).

Weight loss of the litter is related with the nutrient release. Thus, factors that influence weight loss also affect mineralization of nutrients contained in the litter in situations where the release phase dominates the annual decomposition cycle.

10

Summary

The present study was carried out in a protected stand of subtropical evergreen broadleaf forest at Swer (Latitude 25°25.01′ N and Longitude 91°47.47′ E; altitude 1910– 1975 m a.s.l) in East Khasi Hills district of Meghalaya, north-east India. The forest stand has the status of sacred grove and covers an area of 12 ha. The climate of the area is monsoonic with an annual rainfall of about 10,754 mm and mean temperature of 23.5°C measured at the nearest meteorological station at Cherrapunjee. It is a closed canopy forest characterized by high tree diversity, complex community organization and high spatial heterogeneity in species distribution and forest microenvironment. The dominant tree species in the forest were distributed in distinct patches.

Rhododendron arboreum, *Myrica esculenta*, *Symplocos javanica*, *Neolitsea cassia*, *Persea odoratissima*, *Magnolia pterocarpa*, *Engelhardtia spicata*, *Ficus nerifolia*, *Cinnamomum bejolghota* and *Elaeocarpus lancifolius* were dominant/codominant tree species in the forest. *Psychotria symplicifolia*, *Eurya japonica*, *Jasminum dispermum*, *Daphne papyracea*, *Daphne involucrate*, *Ixora subsesillis*, *Tupidanthus calyptratus*, *Viburnum coriaceum*, *Smilax myrtillus*, *Corylopsis himalayana* and *Gleichinia* sp. were abundant among the shrubs. *Ophiopogon intermedius*,

Oplismenus burmannii, *Balanophora diocia* were important herbs in the community.

The relationship between tree diversity and N and P dynamics on the forest floor was intensively studied in 10m×10m permanent experimental plots differing in dominant tree species. Based on the species composition, four types of plots were demarcated viz. plots dominated by (i) *Myrica esculenta*, (ii) *Rhododendron arboreum*, (iii) *Neolitsea cassia*, and (iv) mixed species. The dominant/codominant species in the Mixed plots were *Elaeocarpus lancifolius, Magnolia pterocarpa, Persea odoratissima*. Three replicate plots under each plot category were established and data pertaining to community characteristics, forest microclimate, accumulation, production and decay of litter and fine roots, soil microbial biomass C, N and P and nutrient mineralization at monthly/seasonal intervals were collected during September 2004 to September 2005. The important findings of the study are summarized in Table 10.1.

Table 10.1

Summary of the results obtained in the experimental plots of the humid subtropical forest ecosystem of Meghalaya. Each value is a mean of monthly/seasonal data collected across the year

Parameters	*Experimental plots*			
	Myrica plot	*Rhododendron plot*	*Neolitsea plot*	*Mixed plot*
	1	*2*	*3*	*4*
Structural characteristics				
Tree Density (No. of individuals/ 300m^2)	11^{2}	21^{1}	8^{4}	10^{3}
Tree Basal cover (m^2/300m^2)	1.29^{2}	1.22^{3}	1.07^{4}	1.38^{1}
Tree Canopy cover (%)	73^{3}	79^{2}	81^{1}	81^{1}

(Contd...)

	1	*2*	*3*	*4*
Microclimate				
Light intensity (Lux)	$37{,}213^{1}$	$3{,}215^{2}$	$2{,}495^{3}$	656^{4}
Air temperature (°C)	21.36^{1}	18.90^{2}	18.01^{3}	17.92^{4}
Relative humidity (%)	66.69^{4}	74.92^{3}	79.90^{2}	79.95^{1}
Soil physical properties				
Soil temperature(°C)	16.47^{1}	15.28^{2}	14.89^{3}	14.85^{4}
Soil moisture content (%)	36.49^{4}	44.81^{1}	44.23^{2}	44.07^{3}
Soil chemical properties				
pH	4.36^{4}	4.57^{3}	4.59^{2}	4.64^{1}
SOC (%)	2.69^{4}	3.11^{1}	2.84^{3}	2.88^{4}
TKN (%)	0.59^{4}	0.79^{3}	0.82^{2}	0.89^{1}
Available P (µg g^{-1})	2.57^{4}	3.82^{3}	5.16^{1}	4.07^{2}
NH_4–N (µg g^{-1})	10.22^{4}	11.40^{1}	10.45^{3}	10.49^{2}
NO_3–N (µg g^{-1})	7.24^{4}	8.15^{3}	8.63^{1}	8.39^{2}
PO_4–P (µg g^{-1})	6.57^{4}	7.42^{3}	8.45^{1}	8.42^{2}
Soil biological properties				
MBC (µg g^{-1})	387^{4}	701^{1}	522^{2}	390^{3}
MBN (µg g^{-1})	27^{4}	34^{3}	36^{2}	42^{1}
MBP (µg g^{-1})	7.37^{4}	10.98^{3}	17.10^{2}	17.21^{1}
Soil biological processes				
Nitrification (µg g^{-1} mo^{-1})	8.60^{4}	9.84^{3}	10.45^{1}	10.22^{2}
Net N mineralization (µg g^{-1} mo^{-1})	18.83^{4}	21.88^{3}	22.14^{1}	22.01^{2}
Net P mineralization (µg g^{-1} mo^{-1})	4.54^{4}	5.24^{3}	5.87^{1}	5.74^{2}
Litter				
Mean Accumulation (kg ha^{-1})	5760^{2}	6147^{1}	4544^{3}	4334^{4}

(Contd...)

	1	*2*	*3*	*4*
Annual production (kg ha^{-1} yr^{-1})	$11,732^{2}$	$12,827^{1}$	$11,393^{3}$	$9,535^{4}$
Turnover rate (yr^{-1})	2.04^{4}	2.09^{3}	2.51^{1}	2.20^{2}
Mean N accumulation (kg ha^{-1})	61.77^{1}	49.10^{3}	40.46^{4}	58.83^{2}
Mean P accumulation (kg ha^{-1})	2.05^{3}	2.08^{2}	1.77^{4}	2.60^{1}
Annual N input (kg ha^{-1} yr^{-1})	124.92^{2}	101.33^{4}	103.37^{3}	125.42^{1}
Annual P input (kg ha^{-1} yr^{-1})	4.12^{4}	4.30^{3}	4.67^{2}	5.59^{1}
Litter quality				
N (%)				
Leaf litter	1.27^{2}	0.90^{3}	1.57^{1}	–
Mixed leaf litter	1.23^{3}	1.03^{4}	1.67^{1}	1.63^{2}
P (%)				
Leaf litter	0.043^{2}	0.040^{3}	0.065^{1}	–
Mixed leaf litter	0.032^{4}	0.047^{3}	0.067^{2}	0.070^{1}
Lignin (%)				
Leaf litter	33.21^{2}	35.36^{1}	22.14^{3}	–
Mixed leaf litter	29.42^{2}	37.80^{1}	17.62^{4}	23.37^{3}
C/N				
Leaf litter	37.40^{2}	51.29^{3}	27.81^{1}	–
Mixed leaf litter	47.62^{3}	61.32^{4}	39.70^{2}	28.12^{1}
Decay and mineralization constants				
Leaf litter				
k	0.53^{3}	0.82^{2}	0.89^{1}	–
k_N	0.68^{3}	1.12^{2}	1.39^{1}	–

(Contd...)

	1	*2*	*3*	*4*
k_P	0.62[3]	0.84[2]	0.88[1]	–
Mixed leaf litter				
k	0.59[4]	0.98[2]	1.13[1]	0.85[3]
k_N	0.82[4]	1.25[3]	1.66[1]	1.29[2]
k_P	0.69[4]	0.88[3]	1.07[1]	1.02[2]
Fine roots				
Mean annual drymass (kg ha^{-1})	3,964[4]	4676[1]	4010[3]	4085[2]
Annual production (kg ha^{-1} yr^{-1})	4,320[3]	4,431[1]	4,420[2]	4,297[4]
Turnover rate (yr^{-1})	1.09[2]	0.95[4]	1.10[1]	1.05[3]
Mean N accumulation (kg ha^{-1})	19.03[4]	27.12[3]	48.92[1]	46.97[2]
Mean P accumulation (kg ha^{-1})	0.79[4]	1.87[3]	2.41[2]	2.86[1]
Annual N input (kg ha^{-1} yr^{-1})	20.74[4]	25.70[3]	57.93[1]	49.42[2]
Annual P input (kg ha^{-1} yr^{-1})	0.86[4]	1.77[1]	2.65[2]	3.01[1]
Fine root quality				
N (%)	0.48[4]	0.58[3]	1.22[1]	1.15[2]
P (%)	0.018[4]	0.037[3]	0.059[2]	0.069[1]
Lignin (%)	25.78[1]	24.32[2]	20.77[3]	18.87[4]
C/N	89.50[4]	80.22[3]	37.75[2]	37.54[1]
Decay and mineralization constants				
k	0.33[4]	0.39[2]	0.38[3]	0.45[1]
k_N	0.60[4]	0.78[2]	0.85[1]	0.68[3]
k_P	0.61[2]	0.61[2]	0.57[4]	0.74[1]

The superscripts 1, 2, 3 and 4 denotes the ranking of the experimental plots based on the values in decreasing order i.e., 1> 2 > 3 > 4 of the respective parameters.

Community Characteristics

In *Myrica* plots, *M. esculenta* was the dominant species with 62% canopy cover and 84% basal cover. Similarly, in *Rhododendron* plots, canopy and basal cover was 51% and 77% respectively. In *Neolitsea* plots, *N. cassia* contributed 76% to the canopy cover and 84% to the basal cover. In mixed plots, the tree species together contributed 81% canopy cover.

Forest Microclimate and Soil Characteristics

Air temperature and light intensity were significantly lower inside the forest as compared to the open area outside the forest. The decrease in light intensity was about 59% in *Myrica* plot and 99% in the Mixed plot. The range of variation in ambient temperature between the plots was 2 – 6°C. Relative humidity varied between 67% in *Myrica* plot and 80% in *Neolitsea* and Mixed plots.

Mean soil temperature decreased from 16.5°C (*Myrica* plot) to 15°C (Mixed plot). The soil texture was loamy sand in the *Myrica* plot and sandy loam in the other three plots. The mean soil moisture content (SMC) was high in *Rhododendron*, *Neolitsea* and Mixed plots (44 – 45%) and low in *Myrica* plot (36. 5%).

The soil was acidic in all the plots (pH 4.36 – 4.64) with lowest value (pH 4.36) recorded in the *Myrica* plot and highest in the Mixed plot (pH 4.64). Soil organic carbon content was significantly ($p<0.001$) higher in *Rhododendron* plot compared to the other three plots. The highest concentration of TKN was recorded in Mixed plot. The available phosphorus was highest in *Neolitsea* plot. *Myrica* plots had the lowest soil organic carbon, TKN and available phosphorus contents.

The NH_4^+–N concentration was significantly ($p<0.001$) higher in *Rhododendron* plot (11.40µg g^{-1}) than the other three plots (10.22 – 10.49µg g^{-1}). The variation of NH_4^+–N concentration among the latter three plots was not significant.

The NO_3^-–N concentration did not differ significantly among the plots. However, *Myrica* plot had the lowest value. The PO_4^{3-}–P concentration was significantly higher in *Neolitsea* and Mixed plots than *Rhododendron* and *Myrica* plots.

Litter Dynamics

Input, accumulation and turnover

The highest mean annual accumulation and production of litter was recorded in *Rhododendron* plots followed by *Myrica*, *Neolitsea* and Mixed plots. Its turnover rate was highest in *Neolitsea* plot followed by Mixed, *Rhododendron* and *Myrica* plots.

Nutrient input and accumulation

Maximum N accumulation in litter (61.8 kg ha^{-1}) was recorded in *Myrica* plot and minimum (40.5 kg ha^{-1}) in *Neolitsea* plot. However, its annual input was maximum in Mixed plot (125 kg $ha^{-1}yr^{-1}$) and minimum (101 kg $ha^{-1}yr^{-1}$) in *Rhododendron* plots.

Standing state of P in litter varied between 1.8 and 2.6 kg ha^{-1} with maximum amount in the Mixed plot and minimum in *Neolitsea* plot. Its annual input was maximum (5.6 kg $ha^{-1}yr^{-1}$) in Mixed plot and minimum (4.1 kg $ha^{-1}yr^{-1}$) in *Myrica* plot.

Decomposition and release of nutrients

The decomposition of litter was influenced by its chemical composition, particularly nitrogen and lignin concentration and soil properties such as soil moisture, soil temperature and soil pH. Weight loss of leaf litter was rapid in *Neolitsea* (k= 0.89), followed by *Rhododendron* plots (k= 0.82), and *Myrica* (k= 0.53). Similar trend was observed with mixed leaf litter, but its decay rate was faster than single tree leaf litter (*Neolitsea*, k= 1.13; *Rhododendron*, k= 0.98; Mixed, k= 0.85 and *Myrica* plot, k= 0.59). Mineralization constants of leaf litter were highest in the *Neolitsea* plot (k_N= 1.39 and k_P= 0.88) and lowest in the *Myrica* plot (K_N= 0.68 and K_P= 0.62). Mineralization of mixed leaf litter followed a similar trend but it occurred at faster rate than those of single species leaf litter.

Fine Root Dynamics

Accumulation, production and turnover

Mean fine root drymass was significantly ($p<0.001$) higher in *Rhododendron* plot (4,676 kg ha^{-1}) than the other three plots (3,964 – 4,084 kg ha^{-1}). Similarly, the mean annual production of fine roots was also significantly ($p<0.001$) higher in *Rhododendron* plot (4,431 kg $ha^{-1}yr^{-1}$) than the Mixed plot (4,297 kg $ha^{-1}yr^{-1}$). The most rapid turnover rate was recorded in *Neolitsea* plot followed by *Myrica*, Mixed and *Rhododendron* plot.

Nutrient input and accumulation

Maximum accumulation of N in fine roots was recorded in *Neolitsea* plot (48.9 kg ha^{-1}) followed by Mixed (47 kg ha^{-1}), *Rhododendron* (27.1 kg ha^{-1}) and *Myrica* plot (19 kg ha^{-1}). The annual N input ranged between 20.7 and 57.9 kg $ha^{-1}yr^{-1}$ with minimum value in *Myrica* plot and maximum in *Neolitsea* plot.

P accumulation (0.8 – 2.9 kg ha^{-1}) and input (0.9 – 3 kg $ha^{-1}yr^{-1}$) followed a trend similar to that of N, but their values were much lower than N.

Decomposition and release of nutrients

Decomposition of fine root was slower than the leaf litter. Among the plots, it was most rapid in the Mixed plots followed in decreasing order by *Rhododendron*, *Neolitsea* and *Myrica* plots.

The N mineralization constant decreased from *Neolitsea* plot (k_N= 0.85) to *Rhododendron* (k_N= 0.78), Mixed (k_N= 0.68) and *Myrica* (k_N= 0.60) plots. But P mineralization rate was high in the Mixed plot (k_P= 0.74) and low (k_P= 0.57) in the *Neolitsea* plot.

Microbial Biomass and Nutrient Mineralization

The MBC varied significantly ($p < 0.001$) between the experimental plots and the value ranged from 446 to 922 µg g^{-1} in *Rhododendron*, 347 to 709 µg g^{-1} in *Neolitsea*, 258 to 463 µg g^{-1} in Mixed and 315 to 541 µg g^{-1} in the *Myrica* plots. MBN and MBP also varied significantly ($p < 0.001$) between the plots. Based on these values the plots can be arranged as Mixed ≥ *Neolitsea* > *Rhododendron* > *Myrica*.

The net nitrification and N mineralization rate was slow in *Myrica* plot and fast in *Rhododendron*, *Neolitsea* and Mixed plots. P mineralization rate however, followed the order *Neolitsea*> Mixed> *Rhododendron*> *Myrica*.

Analysis of the above results reveals that the tree species richness had a marked effect on forest microclimatic variables particularly light intensity and relative humidity. Its effect on forest floor was noticed on several physical, chemical and biological properties of the surface layer (0–10 cm depth) of mineral soil. Organic matter and nutrient (N and P) accumulation in litter and fine roots as well as their decay rates and nutrient mineralization processes were significantly altered due to change in composition of tree species. Plots with greater concentration of microbial biomass were associated with higher soil organic matter, high soil pH and high quality of litter. Nutrient transformation processes on the forest floor varied among the plots depending on the distribution pattern of dominant tree species. This may be attributed to change in the quantity and quality of soil organic matter. Considering that the experimental plots are in a steady state condition, where input and output of organic matter and nutrients were almost equal, it may be argued that the difference in the ecological processes observed on the forest floor was related to the differences in the tree species composition and their dominance.

References

Aber, J.D. and Melillo, J.M. 1982. Litter decomposition: measuring relative contribution of organic matter and nitrogen to forest soils. *Canadian Journal of Botany* 58: 416–421.

Aber, J.D., Melillo, J.M. and McClaugherty, C.A. 1990. Predicting long-term patterns of mass loss, nitrogen dynamics, and soil organic matter formation from initial fine litter chemistry in temperate ecosystems. *Canadian Journal of Botany* 68: 2201–2208.

Acosta-Martinez, V., Reicher, Z., Bischoff, M. and Turco, R.F. 1999. The role of tree leaf mulch and nitrogen fertilizer on turfgrass soil quality. *Biology and Fertility of Soils* 29:55–61.

Adams, M.B. and Angradi, T.R. 1996. Decomposition and nutrient dynamics of hardwood leaf litter in the Fernow whole-watershed acidification experiment. *Forest Ecology and Management* 83: 61–69.

Aerts, R. 1997. Climate, leaf litter chemistry and leaf litter decomposition in terrestrial ecosystem: a triangular relationship. *Oikos* 79: 439–449.

Aerts, R. and De Caluwe, H. 1997. Nutritional and plant-mediated controls on leaf litter decomposition of Carex species. *Ecology* 78: 244–260.

Aerts, R. and Chapin, F.S.III. 2000. The mineral nutrition of wild plants revisited: a re-evaluation of processes and patterns. *Advanced Ecology and Evolution* 30: 1–67.

Allen, S.E., Grimshaw, H.M., Parkinson, J.A. and Quarmby, C. 1974. *Chemical Analysis of Ecological Materials.* Blackwell Scientific Publication, London.

Allen, A. S., Andrews, J. A., Finzi, A. C., Matamala, R., Richter, D.D. and Schlesinger, W. H. 2000. Effects of free-air CO_2 enrichment (FACE) on belowground processes in a *Pinus taeda* forest. *Ecological Applications* 10: 437–448.

Anderson, J.M. and Ingram, J.S. I. 1993. *Tropical Soil Biology and Fertility. A Handbook of Methods.* C.A.B. International Wallingford, U.K.

Anderson, J.M. and Swift, M.J. 1983. Decomposition in tropical forests. In: Sutton, S.L., Whitmore, T.C. and Chadwick, A.C. (eds.), *Tropical rain forest: ecology and management.* Special publication no. 2. British Ecological Society. Blackwell, Oxford, pp. 287– 310

Arul Pragasan,L. and Parthasarathy, N. 2005. Litter production in tropical dry evergreen forests of south India in relation to season, plant life-forms and physiognomic groups. *Current Science* 88 (8): 1255–1263.

Arunachalam, A. 1996. The role of litter and fine roots in organic matter and nutrient dynamics during the recovery of degraded subtropical forest ecosystems. Ph.D. Thesis, North-Eastern Hill University, Shillong, India.

Arunachalam, A., Pandey, H.N., Tripathi, R.S. and Maithani, K. 1996a. Fine root decomposition and nutrient mineralization patterns in a subtropical humid forest following tree cutting. *Forest Ecology and Management* 86: 141– 150.

Arunachalam, A., Maithani, K., Pandey, H.N. and Tripathi, R.S. 1996b. The impact of disturbance on detrital dynamics and soil microbial biomass of a Pinus kesiya forest in northeast India. *Forest Ecology and Management* 88: 273–282.

Arunachalam, A., Sarmah, R., Adhikari, D., Majumdar, M. and Khan, M.L. 2004. Anthropogenic threats and biodiversity conservation in Namdapha nature reserve in the Indian Eastern Himalayas. *Current Science* 87: 447–454.

Aubert, M., Bureau, F., Alard, D. and Bardat, J. 2004. Effect of tree mixture on the humic epipedon and vegetation diversity in managed beech forests (Normandy, France). *Canadian Journal of Forest Research* 34: 233–248.

Augusto, L., Ranger, J., Binkley, D. and Rothe, A. 2002. Impact of several common tree species of European temperate forests on soil fertility. *Annals of Forest Science* 59: 233–253.

Ayres,E., Dromp,K.M. and Bardgett, R.D. 2006. Do plant species encourage soil biota that specialise in the rapid decomposition of their litter? *Soil Biology and Biochemistry* 38: 183–186.

Bååth, E. and Anderson, T.-H. 2003. Comparison of soil fungal/bacterial ratios in a pH gradient using physiological and PLFA-based techniques. *Soil Biology and Biochemistry* 35: 955–963

Baillie, I.C. 1996. Soils of the humid tropics. In: Richards, P.W. (2nd edition) *The Tropical rainforest: an ecological study*. Cambridge University Press, Cambridge, U.K.

Balisky, A.C. and Burton, P.J. 1993. Distinction of soil thermal regimes under various experimental vegetation covers. *Canadian Journal of Soil Science* 73: 411–420.

Barbhuiya, A.R. 2006. Role of fine roots and soil microbes in C, N and P dynamics in a humid tropical forest ecosystem of Northeast India. Ph.D. Thesis, North-Eastern Hill University, Shillong, India.

Bardgett, R.D. and Shine, A. 1999. Linkages between plant litter diversity, soil microbial biomass and ecosystem function in temperate grasslands. *Soil Biology and Biochemistry* 31: 317–321.

Barik, S.K., Pandey, H.N., Tripathi, R.S. and Rao, P. 1992. Microenvironmental variability and species diversity in treefall gaps in a subtropical broad leaved forest. *Vegetatio* 103: 31–40.

Barik, S.K., Tripathi, R.S., Pandey, H.N. and Rao, P. 1996. Tree regeneration in a subtropical humid forest: effect of cultural disturbance on seed production, dispersal and germination. *Journal of Applied Ecology* 33: 1551–1560.

Barnes, B.V., Zak,D.R., Denton, S.R. and Spurr, S.H. 1998. *Forest Ecology*. Fourth Edition. John Wiley and Sons, Inc., New York.

Bauhas, J., Pare, D. and Cote, L. 1998. Effects of tree species stand age and soil type on soil microbial biomass and its activity in a southern boreal forest. *Soil Biology and Biochemistry* 30: 1077–1089.

Berendse, F. 1998. Effects of dominants plant species on soil during succession in nutrient-poor ecosystem. *Biogeochemistry* 42: 73–88.

Berg, B. and Ekbohm, G. 1991. Litter mass-loss and decomposition patterns in some needle and leaf litter types. Long-term decomposition in Scots pine forest. VII. *Canadian Journal of Botany* 69: 1449– 1456.

Berg, B. and McClaugherty, C. 2003. *Plant Litter: Decomposition, Humus*. Springer-Verlag, New York.

Berg, B. and Staaf, H. 1981. Leaching, accumulation and release of nitrogen in decomposing forest litter. In: Clark, F.E. and Rosswall, T. (eds.), *Terrestrial Nitrogen Cycles. Ecological Bulletin* (Stockholm) 33: 163–178.

Berish, C.W. 1982. Root biomass and surface area in three successional tropical forests. *Canadian Journal of Forest Research* 12: 699–704.

Binkley, D. 1992. Mixtures of nitrogen-fixing and non-nitrogen-fixing tree species. In: Cannell, M.G.R., Malsolm, D.C. and Robertson, P.A. (eds.), *The Ecology of Mixed-Species Stands of Trees.* The British Ecological Society. Oxford, U.K.

Binkley, D. and Giardina, C. 1998. Why do tree species affect soils? The warp and woof of tree-soil interactions. *Biogeochemistry* 42: 89–106.

Binkley, D. and Menyailo, O. 2005. *Trees Species Effects on Soils: Implications for global Change.* NATO Science Series, Kluwer Academic Publishers, Dordrecht.

Blagodatskaya, E.V. and Anderson, T.-H. 1998. Interactive effects of pH and substrate quality of the fungal-to-bacterial ratio and qCO_2 of microbial communities in forest soils. *Soil Biology and Biochemistry* 30: 1269–1274.

Blair, J.M., Parmelee, R.W. and Beare, M.H. 1990. Decay rates nitrogen fluxes, and decomposer communities of single– and mixed–species foliar litter. *Ecology* 71: 1976–1985.

Bloomfield, J., Vogt, K.A. and Vogt, D.J.1993. Decay rate and substrate quality of fine roots and foliage of two tropical tree species in the Luquillo experimental forest, Puerto Rico. *Plant Soil.*150:233–245.

Boettcher, S.E. and Kalisz, P.J. 1990. Single tree influence on soil properties in the mountains of Eastern Kentucky. *Ecology* 7 (14): 1365–1372.

Bohm, W. 1979. *Methods of Studying Root Systems*, Springer-Verlag Berlin, Heidelberg, New York.

Brookes, P.C., Powlson, D.S. and Jenkinson, D.S. 1982. Measurement of microbial biomass phosphorus in soil. *Soil Biology and Biochemistry* 14: 319–329.

Brookes, P.C., Powlson, D.S. and Jenkinson, D.S. 1984. Phosphorus in the soil microbial biomass. *Soil Biology and Biochemistry* 16: 169–175.

Brookes, P.C., Kragt, J.F., Powlson, D.S. and Jenkinson, D.S. 1985. Chloroform fumigation and the release of soil nitrogen: the effects of fumigation time and temperature. *Soil Biology and Biochemistry*. 17:831–835.

Brüggemann, N., Rosenkranz, P., Papen, H., Pilegaard, K. and Butterbach-Bahl, K. 2005. Pure stands of temperate forest tree species modify soil respiration and N turnover. *Biogeosciences Discussions* 2: 303–331.

Burke, M.K. and Raynal, D.J.1994 Fine root growth phenology, production, and turnover in a northern hardwood forest ecosystem. *Plant Soil* 162:135–146.

Buyanovsky, G.A., Kucera, C.L. and Wagner, G.H.1987. Comparative analyses of carbon dynamics in native and cultivated ecosystems. *Ecology* 68(6): 2023–2031.

Caldwell, M.M. 1987. Competition between roots in natural communities. In: Gregory, P.J., Lake, J.V. and Rose, D.A. (eds.), *Root development and function*. Cambridge University Press. New York, New York, USA. pp. 16–185.

Cardinale, B.J., Nelson, K. and Palmer, M.A. 2000. Linking species diversity to the functioning of ecosystem: on the importance of environmental context. *Oikos* 91:175–183.

Canadell, J. and Rodá, F. 1991. Root biomass of Quercus ilex in a montane Mediterranean forest. *Canadian Journal of Forest Research* 21: 1771–1780

Carney, K.M. and Matson, P.A.2006. The Influence of Tropical Plant Diversity and Composition on Soil Microbial Communities. *Microbial Ecology* 52: 226–238.

Champion, H.G. and Seth, S.K. 1968. *A revised survey of forest types of India.* Government of India Press, Delhi.

Chapman, K., Whittaker, J.B. and Heal, O.W. 1988. Metabolic and faunal activity in litters of tree mixtures compared with pure stands. *Agriculture Ecosystem and Environment* 24: 33–40.

Chavan, K.N., Kenjale, R.Y. and Chavan, A.S. 1995. Effect of forest tree species on properties of lateritic soil. *Journal of Indian Society of Soil Science* 43: 43–46.

Chen, C.R., Condron, L.M., Davis, M.R. and Sherlock, R.R. 2004. Effects of plant species on microbial biomass phosphorus and phosphatase activity in a range of grassland soils. *Biology and Fertility of Soils* 40: 313–322.

Chen, X. 2006. Tree Diversity, Carbon Storage, and Soil Nutrient in an Old-Growth Forest at Changbai Mountain, Northeast China. *Communications in Soil Science and Plant Analysis* 37: 363–375.

Chuyong, G.B., Newbery, D.M. and Songwe, N.C. 2002. Litter breakdown and mineralization in a central African rain forest dominated by ectomycorrhizal trees. *Biogeochemistry* 61(1): 73 – 94.

Condit, R., Hubbell, S. P. and Foster, R. B. 1996. Assessing the response of plant functional types to climatic change in tropical forests. *Journal of Vegetation Science* 7: 405–416.

Conn, C. and Dighton, J. 2000. Litter quality influences on decomposition, ectomycorhizal community structure and mycorrhizal root surface acid phosphates activity. *Soil Biology and Biochemistry* 32: 489–496.

Cornu, S., Luizao, F., Rouiller, J. and Lucas, Y. 1997. Comparative study of litter decomposition and mineral element release in two Amazonian forest ecosystems: litter bag experiments. *Pedobiologia* 41: 456–471.

Cortez, J., Demard, J.M., Bottner, P., Monrozier, L.J., 1996. Decomposition of Mediterranean leaf litters: a microcosm experiment investigating relationships between decomposition rates and litter quality. *Soil Biology and Biochemistry* 28: 443–452.

Côté,L., Brown, S., Paré, D., Fyles, J. and Bauhus, J. 2000. Dynamics of carbon and nitrogen mineralization in relation to stand type, stand age and soil texture in the boreal mixedwood. *Soil Biology and Biochemistry* 32: 1079–1090.

Cotrufo, M.F., Ineson, P., Roberts, J.D., 1995. Decomposition of birch leaf litters with varying C-to-N ratios. *Soil Biology and Biochemistry* 27: 1219–1221.

Couˆ teaux M. M., Bottner, P. and Berg, B. 1995. Litter decomposition, climate and litter quality. *Trends Ecology and Evolution* 10: 63–66.

Cuevas, E. and Medina, E. 1986. Nutrient dynamics within Amazonian forest ecosystems. I. Nutrient flux in fine litterfall and efficiency of nutrient utilization. *Oecologia* 68: 466–472.

Cuevas, E., Brown, S. and Lugo, A.E. 1991. Above and belowground organic matter storage and production in a tropical pine plantation and a paired broadleaf secondary forest. *Plant and Soil* 135:257–268.

De Boer, W. and Kowalchuk G.A. 2001. Nitrification in acid soils: micro-organisms and mechanisms. *Soil Biology and Biochemistry* 33: 853–866.

Dela Cruz, L.U. and Luna, A.C. 1994. Effects of *Acacia auriculiformis* and *Gmelina arborea* on soil and microclimate of a degraded grassland in Nueva Ecija, Philippines. *JIRCAS International Symposium Series* 1:46–54.

De Lucia, E.H., Hamilton, J.G., Naidu, S.L., Thomas, R.B., Andrews, J.A., Finzi, A.C., Lavine, M., Matamala, R., Mohan, J.E., Hendrey, G.R. and Schlesinger, W.H. 1999. Net primary production of a forest ecosystem with experimental CO_2 enrichment. *Science* 284: 1177–1179.

De Moraes, R.M., Delitti, W.B.C. and De Vuono, Y.S. 1999. Litterfall and litter nutrient content in two Brazilian Tropical Forests. *Revista Brasieleira de Botanica* 22: 237–248.

Diaz-Ravina, M., Carballas, T. and Acea, M.J. 1988. Microbial biomass and metabolic activity in four acid soils. *Soil Biology and Biochemistry* 20: 817–823.

Diaz-Ravina, M., Acea, M.J. and Carballas, T. 1995. Seasonal changes in microbial biomass and nutrient flush in forest soils. *Biology and Fertility of Soils* 19: 220–226.

Diaz, S. and Cabido, M. 2001. Vive la difference: plant functional diversity matters to ecosystem processes. *Trends in Ecology and Evolution* 16: 646–655.

Dijkstra, F. A., Hobbie, S.E., Reich, P.B. and Knops, J.M.H. 2005. Divergent effects of elevated CO_2, N fertilization, and plant diversity on soil C and N dynamics in a grassland field experiment. *Plant and Soil* 272: 41–52.

Dudley, J.L., Michener, B. and Lajtha, K. 1996. The contribution of Nitrogen–Fixing Symbioses to Coastal Heathland Succession. *American Midland Naturalist* 135(2): 334–342.

Dutta, R.K. and Agrawal, M. 2002. Effect of tree plantations on the soil characteristics and microbial activity of coal mine spoil land. *Tropical Ecology* 43(2): 315–324.

Dyer, M.L., Meentemeyer, V. and Berg, B. 1990. Apparent controls of mass loss of leaf littermass regional scale. *Scandinavian Journal of Forest Research* 5:312–323.

Ehrenfeld, J.G., Kourtev, P. and Huang, W. 2001. Changes in soil functions following invasions of exotic understory plants in deciduous forests. *Ecological Applications* 11(5): 1287–1300.

Ehrlich, P.R. and Mooney, H.A. 1983. Extinction, substitution and ecosystem services. *Bioscience* 33: 248–254.

Eno, C.F. 1960. Nitrate production in the field by incubating the soil in polythene bags. *Proceedings of Soil Science Society of America* 24: 277–279.

Ewel, J.J., Mazzarino, M.J. and Berish, C.W. 1991. Tropical soil fertility changes under monocultures and successional communities of different structure. *Ecological Applications* 1: 289–302.

Fabiao, A., Madeira, M., Steen, E., Kätterer, T., Ribeiro, C. and Araújo, C. 1995. Development of root biomass in an Eucalyptus globules plantation under different water and new regimes. *Plant Soil* 168–169, 215–223.

Facelli, J.M. and Pickett, S. T. A. 1991. Plant litter: its dynamics and effects on plant community structure. *The Botanical Review* 57: 1–32.

Fahey, T.J. and Hughes, J.W.1994. Fine root dynamics in a northern hardwood forest ecosystem, Hubbard Brook experimental forest, NH. *Journal of Ecology* 82:533–548.

Fahey, T.J., Hughes, J.W., Pu, M. and Arthur, M.A.1988. Root decomposition and nutrient flux following whole tree harvest of northern hardwood forest. *Forest Science* 34: 744–768.

Finzi, A.C., Van Breeman, N and Canham, C.D. 1998a. Canopy tree-soil interactions within temperate forests:

tree species effects on carbon and nitrogen. *Ecological Applications* 8: 440–446.

Finzi, A.C., Canham, C.D. and Van Breeman, N 1998b. Canopy tree-soil interactions within temperate forests: tree species effects on pH and cations. *Ecological Applications* 8: 447–454.

Finzi, A. C., Allen, A. S., Delucia, E. H., Ellsworth, D. S. and Schlesinger, W. H. 2001. Forest litter production, chemistry, and decomposition following two years of free-air CO_2 enrichment. *Ecology* 82: 470–484.

Fisher, R.F. 1995. Amelioration of degraded rain forest soils by plantations of native trees. *Soil Science Society of America Journal* 59: 544–549.

Fogel, R. and Cromack, K.1977. Effect of habitat and substrate quality on Douglas fir litter decomposition in western Oregon. *Canadian Journal of Botany* 55:1632–1640

Fogel, R. and Hunt, G. 1979. Fungal and arboreal biomass in a western Oregon Douglas-fir ecosystem: distribution patterns and turnover. *Canadian Journal of Forest Research* 9:245–256.

FSI 1999. Forest Survey of India, *State of Forest Report,* Ministry of Environment and Forests, Government of India, Dehra Dun.

FSI 2001. Forest Survey of India, *State of Forest Report,* Ministry of Environment and Forests, Government of India, Dehra Dun.

Gallardo, A. and Merino J. 1993. Leaf decomposition of two Mediterranean ecosystems of South West Spain: Influence of substrate quality. *Ecology* 74: 152–161.

Gartner, T.B. and Cardon, Z.G. 2004. Decomposition dynamics in mixed-species leaf litter. *Oikos* 104:230–246.

George, S.J. and Kumar, B.M. 1998. Litter dynamics and cumulative soil fertility changes in silvopastural systems of a humid tropical region in Central Kerala, India. Intl. *Tree Crops Journal* 9: 267–282

Geng, X., Pastor, J. and Dewey, B. 1993. Decay and nitrogen dynamics of litter from disjunct, congeneric tree species in old-growth stands in northeastern China and Wisconsin. *Canadian Journal of Botany* 71: 693–699

Giardina, C.P., Ryan, M.G., Hubbard, R.M. and Binkley, D.2001. Tree Species and Soil Textural Controls on Carbon and Nitrogen Mineralization Rates. *Soil Science Society of America Journal* 65:1272–1279.

Gilbert, O. and Bocock, K.L. 1960. Changes in the leaf litter when placed on the surface of soils with contrasting humus types.II. Changes in the nitrogen content of oak and ash litter. *Journal of Soil Science* 11: 10–19.

Gill, R. and Jackson, R. 2000. Global patterns of root turnover for terrestrial ecosystems. *New Phytologist* 147:13–31.

Gower, S.T. and Son, Y. 1992. Differences in soil and leaf litter nitrogen dynamics for five forest plantations. *Soil Science Society America Journal* 56: 1959–1966.

Grant, R.F. 1994. Simulation of ecological controls on nitrification. *Soil Biology and Biochemistry* 26: 305–315.

Grime, J.P. 1997. Biodiversity and Ecosystem Function: The Debate Deepens. *Science* 277: 1260–1261.

Groombridge, B and Jenkins, M.D. 2000. *Global Biodiversity: Earth's living resources in the 21st century* UK: World Conservation Monitoring Centre. pp 246.

Guerrero, C., Gomez, I., Mataix, S.J., Moral, R., Mataix, B.J. and Hernandez, M.T. 2000. Effect of solid waste compost on microbiological and physical properties of a burnt forest soil in field experiments. *Biology and Fertility of Soils* 32: 410–414.

Haase, R. 1999. Litterfall and nutrient return in seasonally flooded and non-flooded forest of the Pantanal, Mato Grosso, Brazil. *Forest Ecology and Management* 117: 129–147.

Hansen, R.A. 1999. Red oak litter promotes a microarthropod functional group that accelerates its decomposition. *Plant and Soil* 209: 37–45.

Hassink, J. 1994. Effects of soil texture on the size of the microbial biomass and on the amount of C mineralized per unit of microbial biomass in Dutch grasslands soils. *Soil Biology and Biochemistry* 26: 1573–1581.

He, J. -S., Bazzaz, F.A. and Schmid, B. 2002. Interactive effects of diversity, nutrients and elevated CO_2 on experimental plant communities. *Oikos* 97: 337–348.

Hector, A., Beale, A.J., Minns, A., Otway, S.J. and Lawton, J.H. 2000. Consequences of the reduction of plant diversity for litter decomposition: effects through litter quality and microenvironment. *Oikos* 90: 357–371.

Hendrick, R.L. and Pregitzer, K.T.1993. The dynamics of fine root length, biomass, and nitrogen content in two northern hardwood ecosystems. *Canadian Journal of Forest Research* 23:2507–2520.

Henry, M., Stevens, H. and Carson, W.P. 1999. Plant density determines species richness along an experimental fertility gradient. *Ecology* 80(2): 455–465.

Henrot, J. and Robertson, G.P. 1994. Vegetation removal in two soils of the humid subtropics: Effect on microbial biomass. *Soil Biology and Biochemistry* 26: 111–116.

Hobbie, S.E. 1992. Effects of plant species on nutrient cycling. *Trends in Ecology and Evolution* 7: 336–339.

Hobbie, S.E.1996. Temperature and plant species control over litter decomposition in Alaskan tundra. *Ecological Monographs* 66:503–522

Hooper, D.U. and Vitousek, P.M. 1997. The Effects of Plant Composition and Diversity on Ecosystem Processes. *Science* 277: 1302–1305.

Hooper, D.U. and Vitousek, P.M. 1998. Effects of Plant Composition and Diversity on nutrient cycling. *Ecological Monographs* 68: 121–149.

Hooper, D.U., Bignell, D.E., Brown, V.K., Brussaard, L., Dangerfield, J.M., Wall, D.H., Wardle, D.A., Coleman, D.C., Giller, K.E., Lavelle, P., Van der Putten, W.H., De Ruiter, P.C., Rusek, J., Silver, W.L., Tiedje,J.M. and Wolters, V. 2000. Interactions between aboveground and belowground biodiversity in terrestrial ecosystems: patterns, mechanisms, and feedbacks. *Bioscience* 50: 1049–1061.

Hooper, D.U., Chapin III, F.S., Ewel, J.J., Hector, A., Inchausti, P., Lavorel, S., Lawton, J.H., Lodge, D.M., Loreau, M., Naeem, S., Schmid, B., Setälä, H., Symstad, A.J., Vandermeer, J. and Wardle, D.A. 2005. Effects of biodiversity on ecosystem functioning: a consensus of current knowledge. *Ecological Monographs* 75: 3–35.

Huang, Y., Wang, S.L., Feng, Z.W., Wang, H. and Huang, H. 2005. Comparative study of selected soil properties following introduction of broad leaf trees into a clear felled Chinese fir forest. *Communications in Soil Science and Plant Analysis* 36:1385–1403.

Hughes, J.B. and Roughgarden, J. 2000. Species Diversity and Biomass Stability. *The American Naturalist* 155: 618–627.

Isaac, S.R. and Nair, M.A.2006. Litter dynamics of six multipurpose trees in a homegarden in Southern Kerala, India. *Agroforestry Systems* 67: 203–213.

Jackson, R. B., Mooney, H. A. and Schulze, E.–D. 1997. A global budget for fine root biomass, surface area, and nutrient contents. *Proceedings of National Academy of Sciences USA* 94: 7362–7366.

Jain, S.K. and Sastry, A.R.K. 1984. *The Indian Plant Red Data Book.* I. Botanical Survey of India, Department of Environment.

Jamaludheen, V and Kumar, B.M. 1999. Litter of multipurpose trees in Kerala, India: variations in the amount, quality, decay rates and release of nutrients. *Forest Ecology and Management* 115: 1– 11.

Jamir, S.A. and Pandey, H.N. 2003. Vascular plant diversity in the sacred groves of Jaintia Hills in northeast India. *Biodiversity and Conservation* 12: 1497–1510.

Jenny, H. 1980. *The Soil Resource.* Springer-Verlag, New York, New York, USA.

John, B. 1998. Dynamics of fine roots in pine forest ecosystems. Ph.D. Thesis, North-Eastern Hill University, Shillong, India.

John, B., Pandey, H.N. and Tripathi, R.S. 2001. Vertical distribution and seasonal changes of fine and coarse root mass in *Pinus kesiya* Royle ex. Gordon forest of tree different ages. *Acta Oecologia* 22: 293–300.

John, B., Pandey, H.N. and Tripathi, R.S. 2002. Decomposition of fine roots of *Pinus kesiya* and turnover of organic matter, N and P of coarse and fine pine roots and herbaceous roots and rhizomes in subtropical pine forest stands of different ages. *Biology and Fertility of Soils* 35: 238–246.

Jonsson, M. 2006. Biodiversity Loss and the Functioning of Ecosystems. *Ecology. Info.* 30

Joslin, J.D. and Henderson, G.S. 1987. Organic and nutrients associated with fine root turnover in oak stand. *Forest Science* 33: 303–346.

Keyes, M.R. and Grier, C.C. 1981. Above- and below-ground net production in 40-year old Douglas fir stands on low and high productivity sites. *Canadian Journal of Forest Research* 11: 599–605.

Khan, M.L. and Tripathi, R.S. 1989. Effect of soil moisture, soil texture and light intensity of emergence, survival and growth of seedlings of a few subtropical trees. *Indian Journal of Forestry* 12(3): 196–204.

Khan, M.L., Shaily, M. and Kamaljit, S.B. 1997. Effectiveness of the protected area network in biodiversity conservation, a case study of Meghalaya state. *Biodiversity and Conservation* 6: 853–868.

Khiewtam, R.S. and Ramakrishnan, P.S. 1993. Litter and fine root dynamics of a relict sacred grove forest at Cherrapunjee in northeastern India. *Forest Ecology and Management* 60: 327–344.

King, J.S., Pregitzer, K. S. , Zak, D. R., Holmes, W. E. and Schmidt, K. 2005. Fine root chemistry and decomposition in model communities of north-temperate tree species show little response to elevated atmospheric CO_2 and varying soil resource availability. *Oecologia* 146: 318–328.

Knops, J.M.H., Wedin, D. and Tilman, D. 2001. Biodiversity and decomposition in experimental grassland ecosystems. *Oecologia* 126: 429–433.

Knops, J.M.H., Bradley, K.L. and Wedin, D.A. 2002. Machanisms of plant species impacts on ecosystem nitrogen cycling. *Ecology Letters* 5: 454–466.

Konova, M. 1966. *Soil organic matter: its nature, its role in soil formation, and soil fertility*. Pergamon, New York, New York, USA.

Kozlowski, T.T. and Pallardy, S.G. 1997. *Physiology of Woody Plants*. Academic Press, San Diego - London - Boston - New York - Sydney - Tokyo - Toronto.

Lacroix, G. and Abbadie, L. 1998. Linking biodiversity and ecosystem: an introduction. *Acta Oecologica* 19: 189–193.

Lamont, B.B. 1995. Testing the effect of ecosystem composition/structure on its functioning. *Oikos* 74: 283–295.

Lanta, V. and Leps, J. 2006. Effect of functional group richness in manipulated productivity - diversity studies: a glasshouse pot experiment. *Acta Oecologica* 29(1): 85–96.

Lian, Y.W. and Zhang, Q.S. 1998. Conversion of a natural broad-leaved evergreen forest into pure and mixed plantation forests in a subtropical area: effects on nutrient cycling. *Canadian Journal of Forest Research* 28: 1518 – 1529.

Lodhiyal, N., Lodhiyal, L.S. and Pangtey, Y.P.S. 2002. Structure and function of Shisham forests in Central Himalaya, India: Dry Matter Dynamics. *Annals of Botany* 89: 41–54.

L´opez, B., Sabat´e, S. and Gracia1,C.A. 2001. Annual and seasonal changes in fine root biomass of a *Quercus ilex* L. Forest. *Plant and Soil* 230: 125–134.

Loranger, G., Ponge, J.-F., Imbert, D. and Lavelle, P. 2002. Leaf decomposition in two semi-evergreen tropical forests: influence of litter quality. *Biology and Fertility of Soils* 35: 247–252.

Loranger-Merciris, G., Barthes, L., Gardine, A. and Leadley, P. 2006. Rapid effects of plant species diversity and identity on soil microbial communities in experimental grassland ecosystems. *Soil Biology and Biochemistry* 38: 2336–2343.

Loreau, M. 2000. Biodiversity and ecosystem functioning: recent theoretical advances. *Oikos* 91: 3–17.

Loreau, M., Naeem, S. and Inchausti, P. 2002. *Biodiversity and ecosystem functioning: Synthesis and Perspectives.* Oxford University Press, Oxford, UK.

Lovett, G. and Reuth, H. 1999. Soil nitrogen transformations in beech and maple stands along a nitrogen deposition gradient. *Ecological Applications* 9: 1330–1344.

Lovett, G.M., Weathers,K.C., Arthur, M.A. and Schultz, J.C. 2004. Nitrogen cycling in a northern hardwood forest: Do species matter? *Biogeochemistry* 67: 289–308.

Luizao, R.C.C., Bonde, T.A. and Rosswall, T. 1992. Seasonal variation of soil microbial biomass- the effect of clear felling in a tropical rain forest and establishment of pasture in the central Amazon. *Soil Biology and Biochemistry* 24: 805–813.

Luna, A.C., Osumi, K., Gascon, A.F., Lasco, R.D., Palijon, A.M. and Castillo, M.L. 1999. The community structure of a logged-over tropical rain forest in Mt. Makiling forest reserve, Philippines. *Journal of Tropical Forest Science* 11:446–458.

Lugo, A.E. 1992. Comparison of tropical tree plantations with secondary forests of similar age. *Ecological Monographs* 62:1–41.

Madritch, M.D. and Hunter, M.D. 2004. Phenotypic diversity and litter chemistry affect nutrient dynamics during litter decomposition in a two species mix. *Oikos* 105: 125–131.

Madritch, M.D. and Cardinale, B.J. 2007. Impacts of tree species diversity on litter decomposition in northern temperate forests of Wisconsin, USA: a multi-site experiment along a latitudinal gradient. *Plant and Soil* 292:147–159.

Maithani, K. 1996. Microbial nutrient dynamics and mineralization in degraded subtropical forest ecosystems undergoing recovery. Ph.D. Thesis, North-Eastern Hill University, Shillong, India.

Maithani, K., Tripathi, R.S., Arunachalam, A. and Pandey, H.N. 1996. Seasonal dynamics of microbial biomass C, N and P during regrowth of a disturbed subtropical humid forest in northeast India. *Applied Soil Ecology* 4: 31–37.

Maithani, K., Arunachalam, A., Tripathi, R.S. and Pandey, H.N. 1998. Influence of leaf litter quality on N mineralization in soils of subtropical humid forest regrowths. *Biology and Fertility of Soils* 27: 44–50.

Majdi, H. and Persson, H. 1995. Effects of ammonium sulphate application on the chemistry of bulk soil, rhizosphere, fine roots and fine-root distribution in a *Picea abies* (L.)Karst. Stand. *Plant and Soil* 168–169,151–160.

Malmivaara-Lämsä, M. and Fritze, H. 2003. Effects of wear and above ground forest site type characteristics on the soil microbial community structure in an urban setting. *Plant and Soil* 256: 187–203.

Martikainen, P.J. and Palojarvi, A. 1990. Evaluation of the fumigation-extraction method for determination of microbial C and N in a range of forest soils. *Soil Biology and Biochemistry* 27: 797–802.

Martius, C., Höfer, H., Garcia, M.V.B., Römbke, J., Förster, B. and Hanagarth,W. 2004. Microclimate in agroforestry systems in central Amazonia: does canopy closure matter to soil organisms? *Agroforestry Systems* 60: 291–304.

McClaugherty, C.A., Aber, J.D. and Melillo, J.M.1982. The role of fine roots in the organic matter and nitrogen budgets of two forested ecosystems. *Ecology* 63:1481–1490.

McClaugherty, C.A., Aber, J.D. and Melillo, J.M. 1984. Decomposition dynamics of fine roots in forested ecosystems. *Oikos* 42:378–386.

McTiernan, K.B., Ineson, P and Coward, P.A. 1997. Respiration and nutrient release from tree leaf litter mixtures. *Oikos* 78: 527–538.

Mehra, M.S., Pathak, P.C. and Singh, J.S. 1985. Nutrient movement in litterfall and precipitation components for central Himalayan forests. *Annals of Botany* 55: 153 – 170.

Meier, C.E., Grier, C.C. and Cole, D.W. 1985. Below and above ground N and P use by *Abies amabilis* stands. *Ecology* 66: 1928–1942.

Meinzer, F.C. and Goldstein, G. 1996. Scaling up from leaves to whole pants and canopies for photosynthetic gas exchange. In: Mulkey, S.S., Chazdon, R.L. and Smith, A.P. (eds.), *Tropical Forest Plant Ecology*, Chapman and Hall, New York, New York, pp. 114–138.

Melillo, J.M., Aber, J.D. and Muratore, J.F. 1982. Nitrogen and lignin control of Hardwood leaf litter decomposition dynamics. *Ecology* 63: 621–626.

Menyailo, O.V., Hungate, B.A. and Zech, W. 2002. The effect of single tree species on soil microbial activities related to C and N cycling in the Siberian artificial afforestation experiment. *Plant and Soil* 242: 183–196.

Menyailo, O.V., Lehman, J., Carvo, M.S. and Zech, W. 2003. Soil microbial activities in tree-based cropping systems and natural forests of the Central Amazon, Brazil. *Biology and Fertility of Soils* 38: 1–9.

Mishra, B.P., Tripathi, R.S., Tripathi, O.P. and Pandey, H.N. 2003. Effect of disturbance on the regeneration of four dominant and economically important woody species in a broad-leaved subtropical humid forest of Meghalaya, northeast India. *Current Science* 84(11): 1449–1453.

Mishra, B.P., Tripathi, O.P., Tripathi, R.S. and Pandey, H.N. 2004. Effects of anthropogenic disturbance of plant diversity and community structure of a sacred grove in Meghalaya, northeast India. *Biodiversity and Conservation*. 13: 421–436.

Misra, R. 1968. *Ecology Work Book*. Oxford and IBH Publ. Co., New Delhi, India.

Mooney, H.A., Lubchenco, J., Dirzo, R. and Sala, O.E. 1995. Biodiversity and Ecosystem Functioning: Basic Principles. In: *Global Biodiversity Assessment*. Cambridge University Press.

Myers, R.J.K., Palm, C.A., Cuevas, E. Gunatilleke, I.U. N. and Brassard, M. 1994. The synchronization of nutrient mineralization and plant demand. In: Woomer, P.L. and Swift, M.J. (eds.), *The Biological Management of Tropical Soil Fertility* (TSBF). Wiley - Sayce Publications, pp. 81–116.

Morellato, L.P.C. 1992. Nutrient cycling in two southeast Brazilian forests. I Litterfall and litter standing crop. *Journal of Tropical Ecology* 8: 205–215.

Muller Dombois, D. and Ellenberg, H. 1974. *Aims and methods of vegetation analysis*. John Wiley and Sons, New York.

Nadelhoffer, K.J., Aber, P.D. and Melillo, J.M. 1985. Fine roots, net primary production and soil nitrogen availability: a new hypothesis. *Ecology* 66: 1377–1390.

Naeem,S, Thompson, L.J., Lawler, S.P., Lawton, J.H. and Woodfin, R.M. 1994. Declining biodiversity can alter the performance of ecosystems. *Nature* 368: 734–737.

Naeem,S, Thompson, L.J., Lawler, S.P., Lawton, J.H. and Woodfin, R.M. 1995. Empirical evidence that declining species diversity may alter the performance of terrestrial ecosystems. *Philosophical Transactions of the Royal Society London B* 347: 249–262.

Naeem, S., Hakansson, K., Lawton, J.H., Crawley, M.J. and Thompson, L.J. 1996. Biodiversity and plant productivity in a model assemblage of plant species. *Oikos* 76: 259–264.

Naeem, S., Chapin III, F.S., Costanza, R., Ehrlich, P.R., Golley, F.B., Hooper, D.U., Lawton, J.H., O'Neill, R.V., Mooney, H.A., Sala, O.E., Symstad, A.J. and Tilman, D. 1999. Biodiversity and Ecosystem Functioning: Maintaining Natural Life Support Processes. 1999. *Issues in Ecology*. No. 4.

Nambiar, E.K.S. 1987. Do nutrients retranslocate from fine roots? *Canadian Journal of Forest Research* 17: 913–918.

Nayar, M.P. and Shastry, A.R.K. 1988. *Red Data Book of Indian Plants.* Vol – I. Botanical Survey of India, Howrah.

Nayar, M.P. and Shastry, A.R.K. 1989. *Red Data Book of Indian Plants.* Vol – II. Botanical Survey of India, Howrah.

Nayar, M.P. and Shastry, A.R.K. 1990. *Red Data Book of Indian Plants.* Vol – III. Botanical Survey of India, Howrah.

Norgrove, L. and Hauser, S. 2000. Leaf properties, litter fall, and nutrient inputs of *Terminalia ivorensis* at different tree stand densities in a tropical timber food crop multistrata system. *Canadian Journal of Forest Research* 30: 1400 – 1409.

Odiwe, A.I and Muoghalu, J.I. 2003. Litterfall dynamics and forest floor litter as influenced by fire in a secondary lowland rain forest in Nigeria. *Tropical Ecology* 44: 241–248.

Okalebo, J.R., Gathua, K.W. and Woomer, P.L. 1993. *Laboratory Methods of Soil and Plant Analysis: A Working Manual.* Soil Science Society of East Africa.

Technical Publication No. 1.TSBF. Marvel EPZ (Kenya) Ltd. Nairobi, Kenya, pp. 88.

Olson, J.S. 1963. Energy storage and the balance of producers and decomposers in ecological systems. *Ecology* 44: 322–331.

Oostra, S., Majdi, H. and Olsson, M. 2006. Impact of tree species on soil carbon stocks and soil acidity in southern Sweden. *Scandinavian Journal of Forest Research* 21: 364–371.

Ostertag, R. 2001. Effects of nitrogen and phosphorus availability on fine-root dynamics in Hawaiian montane forests. *Ecology* 82(2): 485–499.

Palm, C.A. and Sanchez, P.A. 1990. Decomposition and nutrient release patterns of the leaves of three tropical legumes. *Biotropica* 22: 330–338.

Parker, G.G. 1994. Soil fertility, nutrient acquisition and nutrient cycling. In: Mc Dade, L.A., Bawa, K.S., Hespenheide, H.A. and Hartshorn, G.S. (eds.), *La selva. Ecology and Natural History of Neotropical Rainforest,* University of Chicago Press, Chicago, pp. 54–63.

Parrotta, J.A. and Lodge, D.J. 1991. Fine root dynamic in a subtropical wet forest following hurricane in Puerto Rico. *Biotropica* 23: 343–347.

Parthasarathy, N. 1987. Seasonal dynamics of fine roots in a tropical forest in South India. *Journal of Indian Botanical Society* 66: 338–345.

Parthasarathy, N. 1992. Vegetation, root biology and nutrient cycling. In: Davidar, P. and Parthasarathy, N. (eds.), *Ecological Studies in Agasthyamalai Rainforests, Western Ghats.* Final Technical Report, DoEn Project, Pondicherry University, Pondicherry, pp. 1–31.

Parton, W.J., Schimel, D.S., Cole, C.V. and Ojima, D.S.1987.

Analysis of factors controlling soil organic matter levels in Great Plains grasslands. *Soil Science Society of America Journal* 51:1173–1179.

Peach, K.A. and Tracey, M.V. 1956. *Modern Methods of Plant Analysis*, Vol. I , Springer–Verlag, Berlin.

Perez, C.A., Hedin, L.O. and Armesto, J.J. 1998. Nitrogen mineralization in two unpolluted old-growth forests of contrasting biodiversity and dynamics. *Ecosystems* 1: 361–373.

Persson, H. 1978. Root dynamics in a young Scots pine stand in central Sweden. *Oikos* 30:508–519.

Persson, H. 1982. Changes in the tree and dwarf shrub fine roots after clear cutting in mature Scots pine stand, *Swedish Conifer Forest Research Project Technical Report*, 31: 1–12.

Persson, H. 1983. The importance of fine roots in boreal forests in root ecology and its practical. International Symposium, Gumpensteim A–8952. Irduring, pp. 595–608.

Persson, T. and Wiren, A. 1993. Effects of experimental acidification on C and N mineralization in forest soils. *Agriculture Ecosystem and Environment* 47: 159–174.

Piper, C.S. 1942. *Soil and Plant Analysis*. Hans Publishers, Bombay.

Powers, J.S., Kalicin, M.H. and Newman, M.E. 2004. Tree species do not influence local soil chemistry in a species rich Costa Rica rain forest. *Ecology* 20: 587–590.

Prescott, C.E. 1995. Does nitrogen availability control rates of litter decomposition in forests? *Plant and Soil* 168: 83–88.

Prescott, C.E., Blevins, L.L. and Staley, C.L. 2000. Effects of clear–cutting on decomposition rates of litter and forest floor in forests of British Columbia. *Canadian Journal of Forest Research* 30: 1751–1757.

Priha, O. and Smolander, A.1999. Nitrogen transformations in soil under *Pinus sylvestris, Picea abies* and *Betula pendula* at two forest sites. *Soil Biology and Biochemistry* 31: 965 – 977.

Raich, J. and Tufekciouglu, A. 2000. Vegetation and soil respiration: Correlations and controls. *Biogeochemistry* 48:71–90.

Raich, J.W. and Nadelhoffer, K.J. 1989. Belowground carbon allocation in forest ecosystems: global trends. *Ecology* 70:1346–1354.

Rajendraprasad, M., Krishnan, P.N. and Pushpangadan, P. 2000. Vegetational characterization and litter dynamics of the sacred groves of Kerala, southwest India. *Journal of Tropical Forest Science* 12: 320–335.

Ralte,V. 2004. Impact of shifting cultivation and mining on land degradation and soil biological processes in Nokrek Biosphere Reserve of Meghalaya. Ph.D. Thesis, North-Eastern Hill University, Shillong, India.

Ralte, V., Pandey, H.N., Barik, S.K., Tripathi, R.S. and Prabhu, S.D. 2005. Changes in microbial biomass and activity in relation to shifting cultivation and horticultural practices in subtropical evergreen forest ecosystem of north–east India. *Acta Oecologica* 28: 163–172.

Ramakrishnan, P.S. 1987. Energy flows and shifting cultivation. In: Vinod Kumar, T.M. and Ahuja, D.R. (eds.), *Rural Energy Planning for the Indian Himalayas*. Wiley Eastern, New Delhi, pp.247–276.

Ranells, N.N. and Wagger, M.G. 1996. Nitrogen release from grass and legume cover crop monocultures and bicultures. *Agronomy Journal* 88: 777–782.

Rapp, M., Santa-Regina, I., Rico, M. and Gallego, H.A. 1999. Biomass nutrient content, litterfall and nutrient return to the soil in Mediterranean oak forest. *Forest Ecology and management* 119: 39–49.

Rawat, R.S. 2005. Studies on interrelationship of woody vegetation density and soil characteristics along an altitudinal gradient in a montane forest of Garhwal Himalayas, *Indian Forester* Aug: 990–994.

Reiners, W.A. and Reiners, N.M. 1970. Energy and nutrient dynamics of forest floor in three Minnesota forest. *Journal of Ecology* 58: 497–519.

Reynolds, B.C. and Hunter, M.D. 2001. Responses of soil respiration, soil nutrients, and litter decomposition to inputs from canopy herbivores. *Soil Biology and Biochemistry* 33: 1641–1652.

Rhoades, C.C., Sanford Jr, R.L. and Clark, D.B. 1994. Gender Dependent influences on Soil Phosphorus by the Dioecious Lowland Tropical Tree Simarouba amara. *Biotropica* 26(4): 362–368.

Richards, P.W. 1996. *The Tropical Rainforest: an ecological study*. 2nd edition. Cambridge University Press, Cambridge, U.K.

Rijkers, T., Pons, T.L. and Bongers, I. 2000. The effect of tree height and light availability on photosynthetic leaf traits of four neotropical species differing in shade tolerance. *Functional Ecology* 14: 77–86.

Rhoades, C.C. 1997. Single-tree influences on soil properties in agroforestry: lessons from natural forest and savanna ecosystems. *Agroforestry Systems* 35: 71–94.

Roy, S. and Singh, J.S. 1994. Consequences of habitat heterogeneity for availability of nutrients in dry tropical forest. *Journal of Ecology* 82:503–509.

Roy, S. and Singh, J.S. 1995. Seasonal and spatial dynamics of plant available N and P pools and N mineralization in relation to fine roots in a dry tropical forest habitat. *Soil Biology and Biochemistry* 27:33–40.

Salamanca, E. F., Kancko, N. and Katagiri, S. 1998. Nutrient dynamics in decomposing forest leaf litter: a comparison of field and laboratory microcosm approach. *Journal of Forest Research* 3: 91– 98.

Sariyildiz, T. and Anderson, J. M. 2003. Interactions between litter quality, decomposition and soil fertility: a laboratory study. *Soil Biology and Biochemistry* 35: 391–399.

Sayer, E.J. 2006. Using experimental manipulation to assess the roles of leaf litter in the functioning of forest ecosystems. *Biological Review* 81:1–31.

Schippmann, U., Leaman, D.J. and Cunningham, A.B. 2002. *Impact of cultivation and gathering of medicinal plants on biodiversity: global trends and issues.* Inter-department Working Group on Biology, Diversity for Food and Agriculture, Food and Agricultural Organization of the United Nations, Rome, Italy.

Schlesinger, W.H. and Lichter, J. 2001. Limited carbon storage in soil and litter of experimental forest plots under increased atmospheric CO_2. *Nature* 411: 466–469.

Schmitt, M.A. and Randall, G.W. 1994. Developing a soil nitrogen test for improved recommendation of corn. *Journal of Production in Agriculture* 7: 328–334.

Schulze, E. D. and Mooney, H.A. 1993. *Biodiversity and ecosystem function.* Springer-Verlag, Berlin, Germany.

Scott, N. A. and Binkley, D. 1997. Foliage litter quality and annual net N mineralization - comparison across North American forest sites [Review]. *Oecologia* 111: 151–159.

Seastedt, T.R. 1984. The role of microarthropods in decomposition and mineralization processes. *Annuals Review of Entomology* 29: 25–46.

Seneviratne, G., Van Holm, L.H.J. and Kulasooriya, S.A. 1998. Quality of different mulch materials and their decomposition and N release under low moisture regimes. *Biology and Fertility of Soils* 26: 136–140.

Seneviratne, G. 2000. Litter quality and nitrogen release in tropical agriculture: a synthesis. *Biology and Fertility of Soils* 31: 60–64.

Singh, J.S., Pandey, U. and Tiwari, A.K. 1984. Man and forests: A central Himalayan case study. *Ambio* 3: 80–87.

Singh, J.S., Raghubanshi, A.S., Singh, R.S. and Srivastava, S.C. 1991. Microbial C, N and P in dry tropical savanna: effect of burning and grazing. *Journal of Applied Ecology* 28: 869–878.

Singh, J.S. and Coleman, D.C. 1997. Evaluation of functional root biomass and translocation of photoassimilated 14C in a short grass prairie ecosystem. In: Marshall, J.K. (ed.), *The below-ground system: a synthesis of plant associated processes*. 1. Colorado: Range Science Department series no. 26. Colorado State University, Fort Collins, Colo., pp. 123–131.

Singh, K.P. and Shekhar, C. 1989. Concentration and release patterns of nutrients (N, P and K) during decomposition of maize and wheat roots in a seasonally dry tropical region. *Soil Biology and Biochemistry* 21: 81–85.

Smith, J.H. and Sharpley, A.N. 1990. Soil nitrogen mineralization in the presence of surface and incorporated crop residues. *Agronomy Journal* 82: 112–116.

Smolander, A. and Kitunen, V. 2002. Soil microbial activities and characteristics of dissolved organic C and N in relation to tree species. *Soil Biology and Biochemistry* 34: 651–660.

SoE. 2005. State of Environment, Meghalaya. Department of Environment and Forests, Government of Meghalaya, Shillong.

Spehn, E. M., Hector, A., Joshi, J., Scherer-Lorenzen, M., Schmid, B., Bazeley-White, E., Beierkuhnlein, C., Caldeira, M.C., Diemer, M., Dimitrakopoulos, P.G., Finn, J.A., Freitas, H., Giller, P.S., Good, J., Harris, R., Högberg, P., Huss-Danell, K., Jumpponen, A., Koricheva, J., Leadley, P.W., Loreau, M., Minns, A., Mulder, C.P.H., O'Donovan, G., Otway, S.J., Palmborg, C., Pereira, A.B., Pfisterer, A.B., Prinz, A., Read, D.J., Schulze, E.-D., Siamantziouras, A.-S.D., Terry, A.C., Troumbis, A.Y., Woodward, F.I., Yachi, S. and Lawton, J.H. 2005. Ecosystem effects of biodiversity manipulations in European grasslands. *Ecological Monographs* 57(1): 37–63.

Srivastava, S.K., Singh, K.P. and Upadhaya, S.R. 1986. Fine root growth dynamics in teak (*Tectona grandis* Linn.F.). *Canadian Journal of forest Research* 16: 1360–1364.

Srivastava, S.C. and Singh, J.S. 1989. Effect of cultivation on microbial biomass C and N of dry tropical forest soil. *Biology and Fertility of Soils* 8: 343–348.

Srivastava, S.C. 1992. Influence of soil properties on microbial C, N, and P in dry tropical ecosystems. *Biology and Fertility of Soils* 13: 176–180.

Staaf, H and Berg, B. 1989. Accumulation and release of plant nutrients in decomposing Scots pine needle litter.II. Long term decomposition in a Scots pine forest. *Canadian Journal of Botany* 60: 1561–1568.

Ste-Marie, C. and Par ́e, D. 1999. Soil, pH and N availability effects on net nitrification in the forest floors of a range of boreal forest stands. *Soil Biology and Biochemistry* 31: 1579–1589

Steele, S.J., Gower, S.T., Vogel,J.G., Norman, J.M. and Ryan, M.G. 1997. Root mass, net primary production and turnover in aspen, jack pine and black spruce forests in Saskatchewan and Manitoba, Canada. In : Margolis,H.A.(ed.), *Biosphere atmosphere interactions in the boreal forest Tree Physiology* 17, 8–9, 577–587.

Stephan, A., Meyer, A.H. and Schmid, B. 2000. Plant diversity affects culturable soil bacteria in experimental grassland communities. *Journal of Ecology* 88: 988–998.

Stump, L. M. and Binkley, D. 1993. Relationships between litter quality and nitrogen availability in Rocky–Mountain forests. *Canadian Journal of Forest Research* 23: 492–502.

Sundarapandian, S.M. and Swamy, P.S. 1996. Influence of herbaceous species composition on fine root biomass production in disturbed deciduous forests of Western Ghats in India. *Acta Oecologia* 17: 163–176.

Sundarapandian, S.M. and Swamy, P.S. 1999. Litter production and leaf-litter decomposition of selected tree species in tropical forests at Kodayar in the Western Ghats, India. *Forest Ecology and Management* 123: 231-244.

Sundarapandian, S.M., Chandrasekharan, S. and Swamy, P.S. 1999. Variation in fine root biomass and net productivity due to conversion of tropical forests into forest plantations. *Tropical Ecology* 40: 305–312.

Swamy, H. R. and Proctor, J. 1994. Litterfall and nutrient cycling in four rainforests in the Sringeri area of the Indian Western Ghats. *Global Ecology and Biogeography Letters* 4: 155–165.

Swift, M.J., Heal, O.W. and Anderson, J.M. 1979. *Decomposition in terrestrial ecosystems*. Blackwell Scientific, Oxford.

Symstad, A.J., Chapin III, F.S., Wall, D.H., Gross, K.L., Huenneke, L.F., Mittelbach, G.G., Peters, D.P.C. and Tilman, D. 2003. Long-term and large-scale perspectives on the relationship between biodiversity and ecosystem functioning. *Bioscience* 53: 89–98.

Taylor, B.R., Parkinson, D. and Parsons, W.F.J. 1989. Nitrogen and lignin content as predictors of litter decay rates: a microcosm test. *Ecology* 70: 97–104.

Taylor, L.A., Arthur, M.A. and Yanai, R.D. 1999. Forest floor microbial biomass across a northern hardwood successional sequence. *Soil Biology and Biochemistry* 31: 431–439.

Templer, P., Findlay, S. and Lovett, G. 2003. Soil microbial biomass and nitrogen transformations among five tree species of the Catskill Mountains, New York, USA. *Soil Biology and Biochemistry* 35: 607–613.

Theng, B.K.G., Tate, K.R. and Sollins, P. 1989. Constituents of organic matter in temperate and tropical soils. In: Coleman, D.C., Oades J.M. and Uehara, G. (eds.), *Dynamics of Soil Organic Matter in Tropical Ecosystems*, University of Hawaii Press, Honolulu, pp. 5–32.

Thomas, K. D. and Prescott, C. E. 2000. Nitrogen availability in forest floors of three tree species on the same site: the role of litter quality. *Canadian Journal of Forest Research* 30: 1698–1706.

Tian, G., Kang, B.T. and Brussard, L. 1992. Biological effects of plant residues with contrasting chemical compositions under humid tropical conditions — decomposition and nutrient release. *Soil Biology and Biochemistry* 24: 1051–1060.

Tiedje, J.M. 1988. Ecology of denitrification and dissimilatory nitrate reduction to ammonium. In: Zehnder A.J.B. (ed.),

Biology of Anaerobic Microorganisms. John Wiley, New York.

Tilman, D. and Downing, J.A. 1994. Biodiversity and stability in grasslands. *Nature* 367: 363–365.

Tilmann, D., Wedin, D. and Knops, J. 1996. Productivity and sustainability influenced by biodiversity in grassland ecosystems. *Nature* 379: 718–720.

Tilmann, D., Knops, J., Wedin, D., Reich, P., Ritchie, M. and Siemann, E. 1997. The influence of Functional diversity and Composition on Ecosystem Processes. *Science* 277: 1300–1302.

Tilman, D. 1999. The ecological consequences of changes in biodiversity: a search for general principles. *Ecology* 80: 1455–1474.

Tilman, D., Reich, P.B., Knops, J., Wedin, D., Mielke, T. and Lehman, C. 2001. Diversity and productivity in a long-term grassland experiment. *Science* 294: 843–845.

Trivedi, P. C. 2002. *Ethnobotany*. Aavishkar Publishers. xvi, 455 p. ills.

Upadhaya, K. 2002. Studies on plant biodiversity and ecosystem function in sacred groves of Meghalaya. Ph.D. Thesis, North-Eastern Hill University, Shillong, India.

Upadhaya, K., Pandey, H.N., Law, P.S. and Tripathi, R.S. 2003. Tree diversity in sacred groves of the Jaintia Hills in Meghalaya, Northeast India. *Biodiversity and Conservation*. 12: 583–597.

Upadhaya, K., Pandey, H.N., Law, P.S. and Tripathi, R.S. 2005. Dynamics of fine and coarse roots and nitrogen mineralization in a humid subtropical forest ecosystem of northeast India. *Biology and Fertility of Soils* 41: 144–152.

Upadhaya, K., Pandey, H.N. and Tripathi, R.S. 2006. Effect of disturbance on soil microbial biomass C in sacred groves of Jaintia Hills, Meghalaya. *Indian Journal of Soil Conservation* 34(3): 221–225.

Upadhaya, V.P. and Singh, J.S. 1989. Patterns of nutrient immobilization and release in decomposing forest litter in Central Himalaya, India. *Journal of Ecology* 77: 127–146.

Usman, S., Singh, S.P. and Rao, Y.S. 1999. Fine root productivity and turnover in two evergreen Central Himalayan forests. *Annals of Botany* 84: 87–94.

Valenzuela-Solano, C. and Crohn, D.M. 2006. Are decomposition and N release from organic mulches determined mainly by their chemical composition? *Soil Biology and Biochemistry* 38: 377–384.

Van Rijven, J. and Brendse, F. 2005. Diversity-productivity relationships: Initial effects, long term patterns, and underlying mechanisms. *Proceedings of the National Academy of Sciences of the United States of America.* 102(3): 695–700.

Vance, E.D., Brookes, P.C. and Jenkinson, D.S. 1987a. Microbial biomass measurements in forest soils: The use of chloroform fumigation - incubation method for strongly acid soils. *Soil Biology and Biochemistry*. 19: 697–702.

Vance, E.D., Brookes, P.C. and Jenkinson, D.S. 1987b. An extraction method for measuring soil microbial biomass. *Soil Biology and Biochemistry* 19: 703–707.

Veach, R., Lee, D. and Phillippi, T. 2003. Human disturbance and forest diversity in the Tansa Valley, India. *Biodiversity and Conservation* 12: 1051–1072.

Visalakshi, N. 1994. Fine root dynamics in two tropical evergreen forests in southern India. *Journal of Biosciences* 19(1): 103–116.

Vitousek, P.M., Gosz, J.R., Grier, C.C., Melillo, J.M. and Reiners, W. 1982. A comparative analysis of potential nitrification and nitrate mobility in forest ecosystems. *Ecological Monographs* 52: 155–177.

Vitousek, P.M., Turner, D.R., Parton, W.J. and Sanford, R.L. 1994. Litter decomposition on the Mauna Loa environment matrix, Hawaii: patterns, mechanisms and models. *Ecology* 75: 418–429.

Vogt, K.A., Grier, G.C., Meier, C. and Keyes, M.R. 1983. Organic matter and nutrient dynamics in forest floors of young and mature *Abies amabilis* stands in Western Washington, as affected by fine-root input. *Ecological Monographs* 53(2): 139–157.

Vogt, K.A., Grier, G.C. and Vogt, D.J. 1986. Production, turnover and nutrient dynamics of above- and below-ground detritus of world forests. *Advances in Ecological Research* 15: 303–377.

Vogt, K.A., Vogt, D.J. and Bloomfield, J. 1991. Input of organic matter to the soil by tree roots. In: McMichael, B.L. and Persson, H. (eds.), *Plant roots and their environment*. Proceedings ISSR symposium on developments in agricultural and managed forest ecology, Uppsala, Sweden. Elsevier, Amsterdam, pp 171–190.

Vogt, K. A., Vogt, D.J., Palmiotto, P.A., Boon, P., O'Hara, J. and Asbjornsen, H. 1996. Review of root dynamics in forest ecosystems grouped by climate, climatic forest type and species. *Plant Soil* 187: 159–219.

Walker, L.R. 1993. Nitrogen fixers and species replacements in primary succession. In : Miles, J. and Walton, D.W.H. (eds.), *Primary Succession on Land*, Blackwell Scientific Publications, British Ecological Society: London, U.K.

Wang, A.S., Angle, J.S., Chaney, R.L., Delorme, T.A. and McIntosh, M. 2006. Changes in soil biological activities under reduced soil pH during *Thlaspi caerulescens* phytoextraction. *Soil Biology and Biochemistry* 38: 1451-1461.

Wardle, D.A. 1992. A comparative assessment of factors which influence microbial biomass carbon and nitrogen levels in soil. *Biological Reviews* 67: 321–358.

Wardle, D.A., Zackrisson, O., Hornberg, G. and Gallet, C. 1997a. The influence of island area on ecosystem properties. *Science* 277: 1296–1299.

Wardle, D.A., Bonner, K.I. and Nicholson, K.S. 1997b. Biodiversity and plant litter: experimental evidence which does not support the view that enhanced species richness improves ecosystem function. *Oikos* 70: 247–258.

Wardle, D.A., Barker, G.M, Bonner, K.I. and Nicholson, K.S. 1998.Can comparative approaches based on plant ecophysiological traits predict the nature of biotic interactions and individual plant species effects in ecosystems? *Journal of Ecology* 8: 405–420.

Wardle, D.A., Yeates, G.W., Williamson, W. and Bonner, K.I. 2003. The response of a three trophic level soil food web to the identity and diversity of plant species and functional groups. *Oikos* 102: 45–56.

Wardle, D.A., Yeates, G.W., Barker,G.M. and Bonner, K.I. 2006. The influence of plant litter diversity on decomposer abundance and diversity. *Soil Biology and Biochemistry* 38: 1052–1062.

Wild, A. 1996. *Soils and the Environment: An Introduction.* Cambridge University Press.

Xu, X., Qi, Y., Chen, J. and Song,B. 2004. Scale-dependent relationships between landscape structure and microclimate. *Plant Ecology* 173:39–57.

Xu, X and Hirata, E. 2005. Decomposition patterns of leaf litter of seven common canopy species in a subtropical forest: N and P dynamics. *Plant and Soil* 273: 279–289.

Yamashita, T. and Takeda, H.1998. Decomposition and nutrient dynamics of leaf litter bags of two mesh sizes set in two dipterocarp forest sites in Peninsular Malaysia. *Pedobiologia* 42: 11–21.

Yang, Y.S., Chen, G.S., He, Z.M., Chen, Y.X. and Guo, J.F. 2002. Production, distribution and nutrient return of fine roots in a mixed and a pure forest in subtropical China, Chin. *Journal of Applied Environmental Biology* 8: 223–233.

Yang, Y.S., Guo, J.F., Chen, G.S., Lin, R.Y., Cai, L.P. and Lin, P. 2004a. Litterfall, nutrient return and leaflitter decomposition in four plantations compared with a natural forest in subtropical China. *Annals of Forest Science* 61: 465 – 476.

Yang, Y.S., Chen, G.S., Lin, P., Xie, J.S. and Guo, J.F. 2004b. Fine root distribution, seasonal pattern and production in four plantations compared with a natural forest in Subtropical China. *Annals of Forest Science* 61: 617–627.

Yang,Y.S., Chen, G.S., Guo, J.F. and Lin, P. 2004c. Decomposition dynamics of fine roots in a mixed forest of *Cunninghamia lanceolata* and *Tsoongiodendron odorum* in mid-subtropics. *Annals of Forest Science* 61:65–72.

Yang, Y.S., Guo,J.F., Chen, G.S., Xie, J.S., Gao,R., Li, Z. and Jin, Z. 2005. Litter production, seasonal pattern and nutrient return in seven natural forests compared with a plantation in southern China. *Forestry* 78(4): 403–415.

Zak, D.R., Grigal, D.F, Gleeson, S. and Tilman, D. 1990. Carbon and nitrogen cycling during old-fields succession: constrains on plant and microbial biomass. *Biogeochemistry* 11: 111–129.

Zak, D.R and Pregitzer, K.S. 1990. Spatial and temporal variability of nitrogen cycling in northern Lower Michigan. *Forest Science* 36: 367–380.

Zak, D.R., Tilman, D., Parmenter, R.R., Rice, C.W., Fisher, F.M., Vose, J., Milchunas, D. and Martin, C.W. 1994. Plant production and soil microorganisms in late-successional ecosystems: a continental-scale study. *Ecology* 75: 2333–2347.

Zak, D. R., Holmes, W.E., White, D.C., Peacock, A.D. and Tilman, D. 2003a. Plant diversity, soil microbial communities and ecosystem function: Are there any links? *Ecology* 84(8): 2042–2050.

Zak, D. R., Holmes, W. E., Finzi, A. C., Norby, R.J. and Schlesinger, W. H. 2003b. Soil nitrogen cycling under elevated CO_2 : A synthesis of forest FACE experiments. *Ecological Applications* 13: 1508–1514.

Zar, J.H. 1974. *Biostatistical Analysis*, 2nd edition. Prentice Hall, Englewood Cliff, New Jersey.

Zhang, Q. and Liang, Y. 1995. Effects of gap size on nutrient release from plant litter decomposition in a natural forest ecosystem. *Canadian Journal of Forest Research* 25: 1627–1638.

Zimmer, M. 2002. Is decomposition of woodland leaf litter influenced by its species richness? *Soil Biology and Biochemistry* 34: 277–284.

Zinke, P.J. 1962. The pattern of influence of individual forest trees on soil properties. *Ecology* 43: 130–133.

Index